BE KIND

What kind thing could you do today?

Any act of kindness, however small it may seem, can have an effect. Taking time to listen to a friend, cooking a meal for someone you love, thanking someone who's impacted your life—these simple actions will make you feel good, whether you're the one giving or receiving.

And that's why we, the editors of *Teen Breathe*, have compiled this book. Every month we read articles on the importance of kindness, and how small acts can build together with others to make a difference. We've learned how that chain reaction can travel through your friendships, your school, your community, and around the world.

But it isn't always easy to be kind—to others, or to yourself. It can be hard to know how to help a friend who is sad, annoying when you have to hug a sibling, tricky to tell yourself you did the best you could when you've just messed up. We hope this book will help with all those situations and more, and show you how being kind can make you feel better about yourself, and change the world, one tiny act at a time.

Have courage and be kind

CONTENTS

The power of
KINDNESS

There's a reason that kindness is a major component of the essential teachings of every spiritual philosophy in the world since the beginning of time. After all, kindness is at the heart of so many positive human qualities, including compassion, forgiveness, love, friendship, hope, and generosity. Whether you practice kindness toward others, or are lucky enough to receive the "gift" of kindness yourself, it has an infinite transformative energy

Kindness has become a huge "movement" in the electronic age, despite being generated by a medium that can foster an atmosphere of separateness and aloneness. Today the internet is flooded with heartfelt and well-intentioned ideas from people all over the globe, keen to find ways to practice "random kindness and senseless acts of beauty." This phrase was coined by artist Anne Herbert, who wrote it on a tablemat in a Californian restaurant back in 1982. Bestselling author Jack Kornfield included her story in his writing, promptly launching it into the world and inspiring countless generous actions and selfless good deeds.

BUT CAN YOU BE TOO KIND?

If you spend too much time doing things for others, it may start to feel like other people are draining your well of kindness completely dry. If this is the case, it might be time to take a step back and ask yourself what is really going on. Being aware of the true reason you're giving so much is important. Could it stem from a misguided sense of duty or your own need for approval, rather than simple generosity? Being kind to others is wonderful, but don't forget to be kind to yourself. Do you speak gently to yourself and take good care of you?

An act of kindness a day
Why not keep a record of the kind acts you give and receive over the course of a week and note down how they made you feel? Then simply read them back when you need an emotional "pick-me-up."

"We rise by lifting others"
Robert Ingersoll

KINDNESS: THE ESSENTIALS

* The expression "be kind to your enemies" sums up the very nature of kindness. It acts as a reminder that everyone is part of the same world and, as such, deserves to be treated with kindness and compassion.

* Even the smallest act of kindness can have a profound effect. Aesop, the ancient Greek fable writer, was certainly onto something when he said, "No act of kindness, no matter how small, is ever wasted." Think about a time when you received a warm smile from a stranger when you were feeling low, or someone helped you to carry your heavy luggage, rather than watch you struggle. Both have transformed a negative into something positive.

* Kindness is contagious. When people are kind to each other, a sort of alchemy flows between them. It's a win-win because the person giving and the person receiving both enjoy a feel-good buzz. The receiver leaves the exchange more likely to want to "pay it forward" or to share the generosity to others. And so the magic spreads.

* Kindness is a willingness to full-heartedly celebrate someone else's successes—to be openly happy for the other person. It's a wonderful way to lead a more positive life and get more in return.

* Practicing kindness on a daily basis can transform your view of the world. Those little exchanges all add up, helping to create feelings of trust and safety. We're all in this together and can help each other along the way.

* The heart-opening benefits of kindness will ripple through all aspects of your life. You'll be more mindful of everyone around you and will experience greater feelings of contentment and ease.

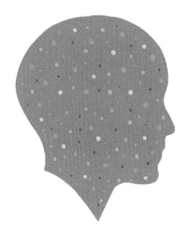

A wonderful world of
DIFFERENCE

Don't fear cultural contrasts—celebrate them

"We are all different but we are all equal" is a motto everyone should strive to live by. The world is full of people of different races, religions, sexualities, and abilities and that's what makes life interesting. Everyone has the right to exist happily as long as they aren't causing harm to others—yet still some people are afraid of those they consider to be different from them. They may mock others who don't share the same interests or because they look different. Sadly, as you may see in the news, some even lash out violently at people with different beliefs and values.

Luckily, most people realize that whatever people's differences, underneath everyone is the same. We are all human, with similar hopes and dreams. Cultural differences are things to be celebrated as there are so many ways they can change everyone's lives for the better.

VIVE LA DIFFERENCE!

Here are a few tips on how you can embrace other cultures while enhancing your own world at the same time…

1 Be curious
At school or at clubs you will be surrounded by many different people and you may hear them talking about an aspect of their life which interests you, such as a religious holiday or food that they eat. If you're sure they're happy to talk about it, ask them questions. No one should be afraid to talk about their differences but sometimes people may find issues difficult or embarrassing to discuss. If you're unsure, approach it in a respectful way, for example: "Do you mind if I ask you about what you mentioned earlier?" If you're worried you'll offend someone, you could always ask your teacher if a question is appropriate.

2 Be open
If you're different in a very particular way from the rest of your class, consider how you might help to educate your peers about it. It could be that you invite them to your home, or bring in food for them to taste. Speak to your teacher to see if you can do something in school to help others understand a different culture. People are curious and want to know but may be fearful of being offensive—try to break the cycle by making the first move.

3 Educate yourself
Other people's histories and traditions can be fascinating. If there's a particular culture you're interested in, look it up on the internet and read about it in novels. Speak to your tutor or student council about holding a diversity day to celebrate the many cultural differences.

4 Learn a new language

Hola! Bonjour! Ciao! How many languages can you speak? You could take on a new challenge and learn new words and phrases from other languages. There are many apps and online videos available to anyone who wants to learn another language. Just choose a language you're interested in and see how much you enjoy it. Learning a few words really can make you feel like you're embracing a fresh world.

5 Play music

You have access to music from across the world on streaming sites such as Spotify™ and Apple Music™, so think about looking at what's in the download charts for different countries and listen to their top 10 singles chart. Hearing the words of songs in other languages is great and a different way to learn. You may even find a new singer you like who no one else has heard of—yet.

6 Hold a movie night

You can find movies from across the world on streaming sites such as Netflix™ and Amazon Prime™. Have you ever watched a Bollywood film or a movie with subtitles? Now's the time to explore the range of movies on offer—or watch a movie about the culture you're interested in. From the comfort of your living room you can easily travel to far-flung destinations.

7 Provide food for thought

Go online to find new recipes from other cultures or ask your parents to order takeout with ingredients that are unfamiliar. To get you started, look for any recipes that you don't normally have at home—they could be Polish, Japanese, Spanish, Irish. Choose anything that's new. You could also ask a friend from a different cultural background for their recommendations.

8 Try something new

Have a look at your local sports center to see what new sports or hobbies you could take up from other countries. You might try a martial art such as karate, or Latin ballroom dancing. You may even want to learn the South Asian board game "carrom." New hobbies help you embrace different cultures, and you may meet new friends too.

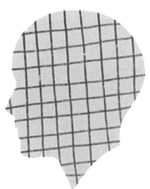

THE ART OF COMPLIMENTS

Telling a friend you admire their style, wish you shared their mathematical brain, or adore the way they use color in their paintings doesn't cost anything and can have a powerful impact. And it can be much more rewarding than you think…

Recognizing the positives about others and sharing our appreciation is a key life skill—it lifts spirits and strengthens relationships. But think also how compliments can make people shine. Best of all, they benefit both parties: The giver becomes a source of happiness while the receiver's self-esteem and motivation gets a boost. But when was the last time you paid a sincere compliment and when did you last receive one?

"Likes" and emojis on social media and texts are, of course, a way of paying a compliment to a friend or family member, but the presence of a screen puts a distance between you and the person you wish to praise. It also tends to remove the sincerity you get from face-to-face conversations, which involve smiles and eye contact. But this lack of personal interaction is just one of the issues. People can be too self-centered to pay attention to what's going on around them. The brain also has a tendency to concentrate on negative experiences, so it's necessary to make a conscious effort to notice positive characteristics in your peers and kin.

Irish playwright Oscar Wilde once said: "It is a great mistake for men to give up paying compliments, for when they give up saying what is charming, they give up thinking what is charming." So be generous and don't withhold praise believing that it will somehow take away your self-worth. The more you perform little acts of kindness, the better you will feel about yourself. And don't forget that expressing gratitude helps to lead to more fulfilling experiences as well as being an effective way to increase your own and other people's happiness.

HOW TO PAY A COMPLIMENT

Complimenting somebody should be as easy to do as a simple pat on the back, but it's still necessary to find the right opportunity to put thoughts into words in an honest manner. Here are simple rules on how to pay a compliment effectively:

Be spontaneous Compliments should come naturally, with no ulterior motives, and should be delivered at an appropriate time. It shouldn't look premeditated, say, as a way of asking for something in return. Don't start telling your dad his new shirt looks great only to ask for a favor a few minutes later. It'll ruin the feeling of sparkle you've just created.

Be observant Paying attention is critical. What makes this person so special and worthy of your praise? Have they improved on a skill, altered their look, or worked hard on something? They will love that you have noticed.

Be specific When expressing your appreciation, look further and comment on something deeper. A vague compliment lacks real meaning and is unlikely to leave a lasting impression. Instead of just saying, "I like your artwork," tell them why. "I like the way you use color in your paintings."

Be sincere A compliment should come from the heart so make sure you mean it and sound like you mean it. "Your hair looks great," can be interpreted in many different ways depending on the tone of your voice.

That said, hold back from too much enthusiasm. Showering someone with too many compliments out of the blue will make you sound obsessed or needy of their affection. It will also more likely embarrass, if not annoy, that so-special person.

HOW TO RECEIVE AND APPRECIATE A COMPLIMENT

If someone tells you how nice you look, how do you respond? Is it with embarrassment, dismissing the compliments with comments like, "No, I don't"? Surprisingly, many people don't know how to take compliments. They tend to discount or ignore them because of a lack of trust in others or their own low self-esteem. Here are a few ways you can learn how to appreciate compliments:

1 Don't be embarrassed
A compliment can be an easy way to start a conversation and break the ice, so when you're paid one, appreciate the comment made. It may be hard for the other person to make compliments so be proud and grateful of their recognition.

2 Accept graciously
Smile, make eye contact, and say a simple, "thank you." No more, no less—it's the polite and contented way to acknowledge a compliment. And the more often you do it, the easier it gets.

3 Don't dispute it…
Rejecting a compliment is like refusing a gift—it can be insulting. Instead, allow yourself to feel proud, forget your modesty, and enjoy being praised for something you have accomplished.

4 …but don't make a big fuss either
Accepting is one thing, agreeing is another. Going on and on about your achievement will make you sound vain and annoying.

5 Cherish it
Everyone needs compliments and praise to build their confidence so it is important to remember such empowering, kind words and, hopefully, others will do the same when you pay them one.

PRAISE BE

Compliments are great, but often they're tied up with what people look like. The good news is there are more meaningful ways to express praise

Almost everybody knows how it feels to have their looks judged—whether it's by boys and girls at school, friends and family, strangers, social media followers, or others in the world. The remarks might be flattering, such as a friend saying you have cool fashion sense or an auntie openly declaring that you have beautiful eyes. Sometimes, though, the observations about your appearance might be unkind and hurtful (this can be particularly true on social media).

Either way, it can give the impression that appearance is the most important thing in life. But there's a way to compliment people that doesn't center on looks. And it might just help to silence any confidence-sapping negative thoughts. Instead, it involves celebrating what makes people different and special. Not sure what to say? Take a look at the list on the right for some ideas and then think about what makes the people in your life stand out from the crowd.

17 WAYS TO GIVE COMPLIMENTS WITHOUT MENTIONING APPEARANCE

1 You're creative
Drawing cartoons, writing stories and poems, customizing sneakers, building treehouses, taking epic photos on your phone—you love getting artistic, super-colorful, and making everything way more exciting.

2 You're brave
Whether it's nailing a big skateboard jump, mastering a muddy mountain bike trail, or making a big presentation in front of the class, you always go for it and do your best.

3 You're a brilliant listener
You know exactly what to do when someone needs a friend. You sit patiently and pay attention, making sure you listen to every single word.

4 You make the best sandwiches
Peanut butter and raspberry jelly, cream cheese and cucumber, chips and coleslaw (there's no judgment here), your bag lunches and after-school snacks are what makes you you.

5 You're confident speaking to adults
You don't mumble, you know loads of interesting facts, you can talk about the weather for at least five minutes (and pretend not to be bored).

6 Your playlists are awesome
Old school rock 'n' roll, indie classics, pop hits, and new songs no one else has even heard of yet, you're the master of music mixes. And you don't keep your discoveries to yourself—you share all the best beats.

7 You give the best hugs
They're not too tight, they're not in awkward positions, they're not too long, they're just nice and comforting. The best bit? When I'm sad, I don't even need to ask for one.

8 You know where to find the best memes
Your Google™ game is seriously strong. It takes you about 20 seconds to find or create the funniest meme for every occasion—laughter is guaranteed.

9 You're caring
You're great at putting other people's feelings first. You always go out of your way to make sure people who need help don't feel alone. You've got a big heart.

10 You're adventurous
Kayaking, diving, rollercoaster rides, windsurfing, ice-skating—you're the first to step up because you think being out of your comfort zone is an awesome way to build your confidence.

11 You always have time for other people
It doesn't matter how busy your study schedule is or how many after-school clubs you're signed up to, you never neglect your friends or family.

12 Parties are better when you're around
If it's not the cool music you're bringing, it's the personality and dance moves. Being brave means you're the first one on the floor—and everyone follows.

13 You can climb any tree

You know the best branches to boost your body up on, the twigs that won't snap, and how to get down in seconds. You've got climbing skills that would make a monkey jealous.

14 You know how to make the perfect bag of sweet treats

Thirty percent gummies, 30 percent sour mix candies, 20 percent milk chocolate, 10 percent white chocolate, 10 percent caramel—the ratios really matter.

15 You have the funniest laugh

Is it a cackle, a guffaw, or a snort? Who knows, but it's infectious.

16 You never waste money on things that don't matter

Your money goes to activities that include friends and family. For you, it's always about making great memories, not splashing the cash on expensive hoodies and jeans.

17 Life wouldn't be the same without you

You're there through the good times, the sad times, the fun times, the tricky times, the boring times—and you make them all 100 times better.

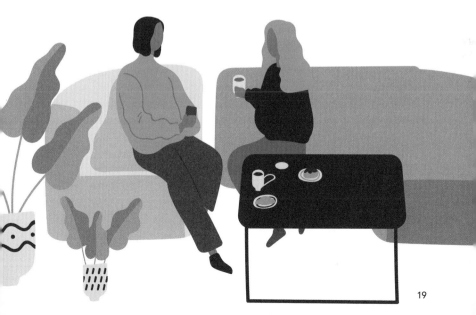

NEW KID ON THE BLOCK

Starting a new school can be a daunting prospect, so think about helping the newbie by making friends with them

Picture the scene: You're the new person at school. Everyone is looking at you as they stand in big groups of friends. All their inquisitive eyes seem to be fixed on you, wondering who you are and what your story is. People are laughing and you're not sure if it's at you but the sound makes you nervous. You're lost, everything is different from your old place, and you feel awkward and alone.

Being the new person is always a scary experience and it takes a lot of courage to start somewhere afresh. What the newbie needs is a friend and hopefully, you'll be the kind, decent person who will help them in their first days and perhaps they will become a really close friend.

While starting a new school is hard, it can feel just as nerve-racking making the first move to welcome someone, especially if you're shy or introverted yourself.

Here are a few tips to help break the ice:

1 Say hello

Think about how horrible it must feel to be alone in a new place, so be brave and introduce yourself. A friendly face and smile will be welcomed. Ask their name and where they are from to start with and offer to show them where the important places are such as the restrooms and the cafeteria. Be the kind of friend you would want in that situation.

2 Find common ground

Conversations may be awkward at first until you get to know them better and it's best not to ask personal questions about their past or why they've joined your school until you bond. Instead, try to find things you have in common so you have something to talk about. Open-ended questions that don't just have a "yes" or "no" answer are best. For example, "What kind of music do you like?" or "What is your favorite TV show?" Or perhaps discuss something that's happening in the news right now or on social media.

3 Pay a compliment

Find something positive you can say to the new person to make them feel more relaxed. For example, they may have a nice bag, shoes, or hair—or if you're in class, perhaps they have good ideas or handwriting. They will really appreciate your attempts to make them feel at ease. It will also make you feel good knowing you're doing a positive thing.

4 Avoid being in a clique

Some teenagers are part of what is called a clique—a group of friends who don't let anyone else join them. Instead of being in a clique, you should invite the new person to join you and your friends for lunch or to go out in the evening to help them get to know new people. Imagine what you'd like to happen to you if you started somewhere new.

5 Try connecting on social media

One of the biggest things students have in common is having an Instagram™ or Snapchat™ account, so why not break the ice by asking for their contact details? You can then text them and invite them to events or ask them how their day was, although it may be best to avoid texting too much to start with. Sometimes, it's easier to talk to people through your phone because long silences don't matter.

6 And if they don't respond or don't seem to want to be friends?

Despite all your good intentions, you may find the new student just isn't interested in conversation or making friends and it could be for many reasons. They could be shy or distrustful or simply very different from you. If they don't want to be friends at this stage, then know it has nothing to do with you. You're the decent one making an effort and have done something good and brave. At least you tried.

LISTEN UP

Are you a good listener? How do you know? Being listened to properly can make you feel valued and appreciated, but doing it well isn't as easy as you might think...

Have you ever had the feeling that someone was really listening to you? That they "got" you and understood where you were coming from? Do you remember how good that felt? Perhaps it was a teacher who recognized your talent for their subject, or an aunt or family friend who took the time to hear your point of view.

Taking time to listen

In a world full of noise and chatter, listening is an underrated skill. People feel desperate to talk and be heard by others, and they may not put so much emphasis on taking their turn to listen. There may be times when you don't feel like listening, like when a teacher is lecturing you about a subject you're not interested in, or when a parent is telling you off. It can be especially hard to feel like listening when you haven't been properly heard yourself.

With friends, listening can be an act of generosity. Not just for the person being heard, but for you too. It allows you to take a vacation from your own concerns, and to help a friend through theirs. It can help to build trust and deepen friendships.

SO WHAT DOES IT TAKE TO
BE A GOOD LISTENER?

Here are some tips:

1 Keep things confidential
When you hear something interesting, shocking, or exciting, it can be tempting to go and talk about it to a friend. Another person's private life can seem like a juicy conversation topic, and everybody gossips from time to time. But being a good listener is about being a trusted confidant. If you keep your friends' secrets safe, they are more likely to confide in you.

2 Don't interrupt
Have you noticed how often people tend to interrupt each other? One person starts talking then another jumps right in. Spend a day listening to the conversations around you and notice how much people interrupt. You might be surprised how often people can barely finish their sentences before someone else begins theirs.

Next time you are having a conversation, try to be mindful of letting people finish their own words before you speak. Being patient and allowing someone to get to the end of what they are saying is a great (and rare) listening skill.

3 Don't give advice
When people talk about their problems, others tend to give advice, or offer solutions to fix them. Often advice-giving is more about the giver than the receiver. People want to feel like they are clever and can think of solutions and they forget that the person they are listening to is the best expert on their own life.

When people are upset, they can't always think clearly and need to offload those emotions. If someone is talking fast, or dealing with a strong feeling, they need to be listened to without advice. When you listen without giving views or suggestions, you can help the person talking to release their feelings. Once they have lightened their own emotional load, they may well be able to come up with a solution for themselves.

4 Be okay with emotions

When you were younger, did anyone ever call you a cry-baby? Did you find that adults sometimes became frustrated with you when you were upset, when what you really needed was kindness and empathy? Although people sometimes feel uncomfortable with tears, crying is actually a healthy and natural healing process. The stress hormone cortisol is released through tears. One of the kindest things you can do for a friend is just to be okay with their emotions.

5 Use your listening skills wisely

Although there are benefits to listening, it can sometimes be draining. People can become so wrapped up in their own problems, they may not be considerate of how you feel, or if you need to talk about your issues too.

Remember that listening skills should be used wisely and only when you have the energy. You don't want to find yourself in a situation where conversations are often one-way and only based on someone venting to you about their problems. Imagine that your listening energy is like a cup full of liquid. It can quickly drain away when you don't have anyone listening to you, or to fill your cup back up again. Conversations need to be balanced.

6 Listening buddies

A good way to make things fair is to enter into a listening partnership. This is when two people set up an agreement to take turns to talk and listen about how their lives are going. You can set a timer, it could be for 10 minutes to start. One person can talk while the other listens and when the timer is up you can restart it and swap turns.

Before you start be sure to agree to keep everything confidential, and also not to talk to each other later about what was said during the session. This creates a safe space, so the other person only talks about their problem at a time of their choosing.

When the listening session ends, ask your buddy a question about something mundane and everyday. Maybe try something like: "What animals can swim?" or "What did you have for dinner last night?" This will help your friend turn their attention away from their problem, and bring them back to reality.

FRIENDS REUNITED

Good friends can provide you with fun times and support, so when you argue with one of them it can impact your life. You might go through a range of emotions such as upset, anger, disappointment, worry, and also loneliness as you miss your friend being in your life. But if you want to mend the relationship with this person, what can you do?

MENDING YOUR RELATIONSHIP

1 Reflection time
Think back to how the fallout started. Is this a one-off argument or something that's been happening a lot? It could be that your friend was having a bad day or experiencing a hard time at home. Consider their point of view—could you be in the wrong? Or have they misunderstood something? Talk to someone you trust and who is honest with you about what has gone on and ask their opinion.

2 Calm down
Find time to calm down and think things through. That doesn't just mean not seeing that person, it means not texting either. When you're annoyed, it's easy to say, do, or write things in anger that you might come to regret. Get rid of the anger by telling someone you trust or write it down in a journal. It's important to give your friend space, too, and let them think about what's happened.

3 Resolve it quickly
You may have heard the saying about never going to bed angry so you have a fresh start in the morning. If you want to avoid a sleepless night, when you feel calm again, try calling or texting to straighten things out. It may be you need a few days to think, but don't leave it too long or making up can become harder. Life is too short to argue and the quicker you can get back to normal, the happier you will be.

4 Choose your words

When you're discussing what happened, it's important to be calm and try not to say anything hurtful that might cause more drama or lead to even more arguing. Explain how fighting with them upsets you. Using "I feel…" sentences such as "I feel anxious when you ignore me" or "I feel worried when you send angry texts" are better than accusatory "you" statements such as, "You are always snappy." If you really can't speak to your friend, or they won't talk to you, perhaps an honest, genuine letter could be the best answer.

5 Say sorry

It can be hard to be the one to make the first move but if you were at fault, apologize and take responsibility for what you said or did. Even when you think the other person is wrong, you could say, "I'm sorry if you feel that way" or "I'm sorry if I upset you." If they are a true friend, they'll react positively. If you find it hard saying sorry, practice in front of a mirror. A small, thoughtful gift or homemade card might help repair your friendship too.

6 Make a pact

Before the end of the chat, talk about how you can stop this happening again. Ask them to speak to you rather than getting moody, or agree to be honest at all times. You could try, "If I feel you are leaving me out, I will speak to you." You may have learned something about how your friend reacts in certain situations or what it is that triggers their annoyance, and these things will be easier to avoid in the future. Either way, now's the time to move on, leave the bad memories in the past, and enjoy your friendship again.

7 Talk it out

If you can, meet in a neutral place where you can talk without the risk of being interrupted. Even though it's a scary prospect, talking things through, face-to-face, is the best way to resolve conflicts. Listen to the other person and try to see their point of view without interrupting or arguing. If they apologize, accept it graciously. If you don't agree with what they're saying, could you agree to disagree? Either way, tell them you value their friendship. If you are worried how your friend will react, having a mutual friend there when you meet could help you resolve things more amicably.

8 And if things go wrong?

If you did something wrong and your friend cannot accept your apology or doesn't want to be friends despite your efforts, there's not too much you can do. It will hurt for a while, but focus on your other friends and remain mature and polite when you see your old friend. Chances are they'll probably want to be friends again when they have had more time to reflect. If they don't, it's their loss. Be proud of yourself for trying.

"The most beautiful discovery true friends make is that they can grow separately without growing apart"

Elisabeth Foley

WHOSE SIDE
ARE YOU ON?

Being part of a group of close-knit friends is great fun... until a couple of your pals argue and you're stuck in the middle of their squabbling. When two people you care about fight, it can put you in a difficult situation and place an enormous amount of pressure on you. But there are ways for you to deal with it to ensure you remain friends with both, avoid stressful situations, and, hopefully, help them make up and move on

HOW TO PLAY PEACEMAKER

1 Stay neutral
If your friends are in a disagreement, it doesn't mean they have to split up with you, too. Their conflict shouldn't affect your relationship with them, so remind everyone that you're there for both of them and this won't change. If they're good friends, they'll respect you for staying loyal to both of them.

2 Avoid pressure
During arguments, insecure friends can sometimes react selfishly and may even demand you only remain friends with them. If they do this, they'll be putting you in a difficult situation. A good friend won't try to emotionally blackmail you or intimidate you to be disloyal to anyone else.

3 Listen without prejudice
You might not agree with their opinions, but take time to listen if they want to talk about the fight. It would be easy to say you don't want to hear it and wish to stay out of the debate, but for some, talking is their way to move forward and release pent-up emotions. If they ask your opinion, don't start being mean about the other person or agree with any negative comments. It'll end badly for you when they make up. Instead, try to find a way to help them resolve the issue, but insist you aren't there to take sides.

4 Respect their decision
While it may be tempting to try to get them to quickly make up, respect that they may not be ready for that even though it would make your life easier. Avoid forcing them to talk to each other or having to hang out together if they need time and space to fully process what's happened. Sometimes they may just need breathing room to realize their mistakes and hopefully they'll be able to reconcile themselves without your input.

5 Don't be the messenger
Avoid stressful situations that may be caused by agreeing to pass messages between the two. You'll be the one who ends up caught in the arguments and being dragged into their disputes—and probably receive criticism yourself if the message is misunderstood. If you're asked to take on the role of a go-between, suggest they find a way to communicate with each other directly or offer to be a mediator between them.

6 Attempt reconciliation

If you think it might work, and it's the right time, encourage them to make up. Ensure you have a good understanding of what's happened before getting involved. Often problems are caused by misunderstandings—can you point this out? Is it a petty argument that quickly got out of hand? Sometimes, people need reminding that life is too short for arguments and it may make them question whether it's worth arguing.

7 Be the mediator

Arrange for your friends to meet with you at a neutral place. Acting as the mediator in the middle, try to make them see you're there to help everyone to move forward because you want them to be friends. Suggest guidelines about speaking, raising voices, respecting each other, and give each person time to talk. See if you can work out a way for them to forgive, apologize, and move on. If you can't, at least you tried.

8 Focus on behavior—don't make it personal

Sometimes it may be that you disagree with a friend's comments or behavior. Depending on your relationship, you may be able to make them realize what they've done and encourage them to apologize. To avoid conflict, when you speak to them, focus on their behavior and what they've done rather than getting personal and criticizing them or being judgmental. Communicating in a calm, polite, and kind way will hopefully inspire them to do the same.

9 Be patient

It's hard to be patient when it's a tense situation, but accept they may not make up quickly. If you struggle with the mediation, seek advice from other friends or speak to both parties to see what they want to happen. If they're true friends, they will get over any small arguments with or without your help. Friendships and friendship groups change many times throughout life so it could be their relationship wasn't meant to be. What's most important is you surround yourself with healthy, positive people who realize you're a really good friend.

FIGHTING FAIR

If you know anyone long enough, there will come a time when you argue. But fights with friends need to be helpful, not hurtful. They need to end with both of you feeling like the other person still cares, but that you've aired your grievances and can move past them. Here are some top tips:

* Don't call them mean names or say something to make them feel bad just for the sake of it.

* Try writing things down in a journal to understand your feelings better before raising a thorny issue.

* Focus on talking about what it is they're doing that's upset you, rather than the kind of person they are.

* Don't make threats or start plotting your revenge!

* It can be helpful to understand exactly what it is you hope will happen. Is there something they can do to fix the situation? Then tell them.

* Don't pretend to be more upset than you are. You need to be honest if you're going to remain friends.

* Be prepared to compromise—spend time thinking about what the other one may be feeling and why.

* There's no need to keep referring back to it once you've each had your say and things have calmed down—if you aren't satisfied, say so, but be as constructive as possible.

* Remember you care about them and remind them of that too—"You're my best friend, but you're upsetting me by…"

SHOULD YOU FORGIVE?

It may have been a betrayal, a lie, a mean joke. Whatever the reason, most people have faced the question of whether to forgive someone

Understanding how forgiveness works

Why is it sometimes hard to forgive? The journey to forgiveness can be difficult and it's not simply about pretending that nothing happened. Forgiveness is about moving on from a situation that hurt you so deeply you may have had to re-evaluate the relationship with the person who wronged you. This is no easy task given it's often close friends or family members who have the capacity to inflict the biggest emotional blows. So whether it was rejection, deception, or ridicule, granting forgiveness involves fully processing your emotions to be at peace again because the act of forgiveness actually takes place in your own mind—in fact, it has nothing to do with the other person. And true forgiveness will also free you of the pain.

Why it's important to forgive

Try not to see forgiving as a weakness or feel that it means you have to forget an upsetting incident. Instead, it is an active, empowering decision to let go of the negative emotions of sadness, blame, anger, or resentment that flood the body with stress hormones and lead to health problems, such as headaches, bad digestion, poor sleep, and skin conditions. Being unable to forgive tends not to harm the other person as much as it does you. So, regardless of how valid your reasons for having these feelings of hurt and confusion, it might still help to move beyond them and embrace peace. Being able truly to forgive those who have wronged you is powerful and can help give you a greater understanding of and compassion for those around you.

STEPS TO FORGIVENESS

1 Talk about it
Talking doesn't mean gossiping and getting back at the person by destroying their reputation. But discussing what happened with a trusted friend might help you to see the situation differently and express how you feel.

2 Write about it
The aim is not so much about finding reconciliation with the person who hurt you but more about clearing the mental clutter and the grudge you hold against them. Writing your feelings down on paper will allow you to be honest with yourself and explore your motivations.

3 Let go of the past
Replaying painful events and reliving hurtful moments will only result in angry or distressed thoughts at bedtime. Most people have a habit of reviewing the day's negative events just before they go to sleep. Try to concentrate on the good things instead—it will make sleep come more easily.

4 Accept and move on
Stop dwelling on what happened. You can't change it, so accept it as being in the past. If you insist on holding onto it, then you will never be free. "Close the door" and walk forward. You have survived and will emerge stronger.

happiness

WHAT IS PREJUDICE?

Have you ever formed an opinion about someone even though you don't actually know anything about them?

Perhaps you think the new girl in school is boring because she's shy or that the well-spoken lady you've overheard must be snooty or that the man whose job is to pick up litter every day can't have any qualifications.

When a person forms assumptions about someone (or something) and forms a bias without having any prior knowledge, experience, consideration, or understanding, this is called prejudice. Everyone has done it at some point—it's part of being human.

The most common prejudices relate to religion, race, sexuality, social class, culture, disability, age, and appearance. People can be prejudiced about someone because of the way they look or the type of clothes they wear or because they have different ideas and interests.

Although a prejudgment can be well-intended in some cases (for example, saying that a tall person must be naturally good at basketball), most prejudices form ideas, attitudes, feelings, or opinions that are unreasonable, unfair, and potentially damaging because they're based on opinion, not fact.

Why do people prejudge?

It's easy to make assumptions about someone or something before knowing the facts. Most people are curious and imaginative and can sometimes try to suss out a newcomer or a situation without knowing the true details. The problem comes when those ideas escalate and form prejudgments.

At some point in life, everyone experiences prejudice—either by prejudging or being prejudged—and this is often born out of distorted viewpoints, ignorance, perceived differences, and fear of the unknown.

Society and the media can drive these distorted viewpoints by creating stereotypes (a fixed idea of a particular type), which can foster more prejudice. For example, people who enjoy science can be stereotyped as nerds while hoodie-wearing youths that hang out in groups must be gang members. Prejudice can also stem from family beliefs. If your parents have a strong bias against certain people, groups, ideas, or lifestyles, for instance, this can easily be passed down and influence your view of the world.

Consequences of prejudice

For those on the receiving end of prejudice, the experience can severely impact their sense of well-being. It can make people feel sad, hurt, frightened, isolated, and excluded. There is also a cost to those who are making these prejudgments. For example, if you avoid someone or something as a result of your prejudice, you can actually lose out on what could be an incredible friendship or an amazing experience.

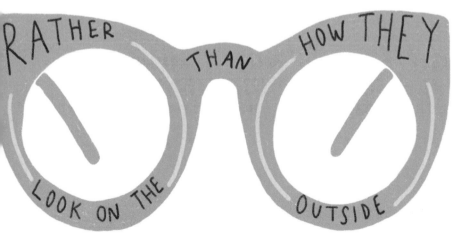

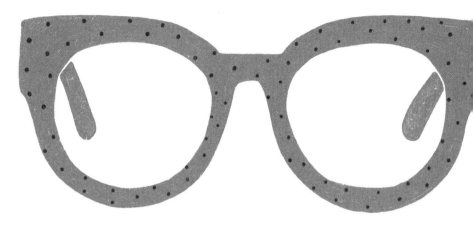

When prejudice goes too far

When people act on their prejudice, this can result in discrimination, intolerance, bullying, and even hate crimes. You don't have to look far back in history to see how prejudice can intensify into the likes of racism, sexism, nationalism, homophobia, or xenophobia. Prejudice against Native Americans, for example, caused them to be persecuted and driven from their homes and land.

In some parts of the world, women were denied the right to vote, while schools and public places were segregated, or separated, by race and the color of someone's skin. Wars have started and, in some cases, still rage as a result of making prejudgments without facts.

Sadly, prejudice and discrimination of one type or another continues to be prevalent in many parts of the world.

Prejudice in your life

Can you identify where there might be prejudice in your own life? What a person is like on the inside can't always be seen on the outside. Are you making prejudgments about people, things, and situations without knowing the facts? Do you feel that people—even family, friends, teachers, or peers—are making assumptions about you without being aware of the true story? Are you witnessing prejudice against others?

By identifying and being mindful of prejudice for what it is—merely an assumption and prejudgement without any substance—you can change your attitude to prejudice and start to lead by example.

HOW TO COMBAT PREJUDICE AND WHAT TO DO IF YOU EXPERIENCE OTHERS' ILL-INFORMED ATTITUDES

What to do if it happens to you

* Speak about your experience to someone you trust—perhaps a teacher, a mentor, or someone in your family.

* Know and accept yourself. Be proud of who you are regardless of what others might think about you.

* Join an inspiring and uplifting group of like-minded people.

* Find an expressive outlet for your emotions through art, music, writing, dance, and other creative activities.

* Make a difference by talking about prejudice and being active in reducing discrimination through public awareness.

How to stop prejudging

* Be mindful of your thoughts, attitude, and behavior especially when meeting new people or experiencing new situations.

* Educate yourself about people, cultures, and circumstances before forming any opinions.

* Try to show more empathy, consideration, fairness, and understanding. See people for who they are inside rather than how they look on the outside.

* Stop to think. Don't be easily influenced by others' opinions. Consider a situation from all sides and choose words carefully.

* If you are tempted to prejudge, imagine being in the same situation and how it would feel.

* Speak out against prejudice.

STOP THE SQUABBLING

Why you should avoid getting into arguments on social media—and how to handle the situation if you do

Ask students or teachers what kind of problems they deal with more than any other and they will tell you two words: social media. While there are many positive and fun things about Snapchat™, Instagram™, Facebook™, and other apps, when arguments start, they can get very nasty, very quickly. What's more, it's hard to take things written down back as they can be screen-grabbed and shared with others quickly.

In comparison to communicating with those you know in real life, some people find themselves constantly getting into heated debates on internet forums. While arguments face to face are often intense and over quickly, social media arguments can go from bad to worse rapidly. They can also continue for days because of miscommunication and some people find they have more courage to say aggressive and hurtful comments from behind the safety of a keyboard or phone.

Here's a quick guide to handling arguments online and how to avoid them in the first place:

1 Choose your words—and your emojis—wisely

When you have an argument or debate with a person in the same room as you, you get to see facial expressions, body language, and hear their tone of voice, so it's easy to see how the other person feels, whereas text messages can easily be misinterpreted. An innocent post can be taken the wrong way so it's really important to choose your words wisely and to think about what punctuation, emojis, or GIFs you use to accompany it to create the right tone.

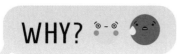

2 Think before you speak

Whether responding to an angry text or an emotive post on a forum, take time before replying when you're annoyed. It's easy to make comments you'll regret when you're upset so try leaving your response for a few hours or speak to someone you trust and ask their advice on how to reply. A different perspective from someone outside the group can help you see a situation from another angle.

3 Stop the argument

Sometimes you'll have to admit that you'll never agree on a subject and stop the argument, whether it's on a group forum or with a friend. If it's a situation where you can see that you won't be able to change people's opinions, just agree to disagree.

4 Talk it out

If it's an argument with a friend, ask to meet to talk to them in person. It takes a brave person to do this, but it's better to resolve the situation quickly. Social media arguments could go on for days, give rise to confusion, and cause a lot more anxiety. Perhaps send a text saying, "Can we meet to sort this out?" or even chat to them on the phone.

5 Ignore keyboard warriors

A negative aspect of social media is the trolls and aggressive posters who get pleasure from posting nasty comments. If you fall victim to an anonymous poster's cruel comments, you can either choose to respond (which is what they want) or ignore them and, if appropriate, report them on the site. The best response is to refuse to communicate with them. They will get bored and (sadly) move on to someone new.

6 Speak out

If an argument is really bothering you and you can't resolve it, speak to a family member, friend, or teacher and tell them how it's affecting you. If it's with a friend, a trusted adult might be able to mediate between the pair of you, and if it's with a stranger, they should be able to advise you how to handle it.

7 Resist the urge

If someone is making snarky comments on an internet forum, why worry about them? They don't know you and you'll probably never meet them. Just try to accept that while they may seem wrong, there are more important things to worry about than a stranger with opposing ideas.

HATE IS A BIG WORD...

...and an even stronger emotion. Whether you're on the receiving end of someone's hatred or struggling with such feelings yourself, there are ways of turning it around

Do you often use the "h" word? "I hate spiders," "I hate peas," "I hate reality television." These are all harmless statements, often delivered in a casual way, but what happens when such feelings become more than a straightforward dislike and are targeted at another individual or group of people?

What is hate?
Hatred is strong feelings of anger, hostility, or resentment toward another person or group. It might even lead to prejudice, discrimination, bullying, or violence.

What does it feel like?
An individual who hates might fixate on their enemy, getting pleasure from thoughts of humiliating them or gaining revenge. It can lead to a dark mood, poor judgment, and irrational thoughts. Some people might bully, exclude, or spread malicious gossip about the target of their hatred.

Why do people hate?
Some negative attitudes might be picked up from friendship groups, family, or the media. If those around you have strong negative feelings toward a person or group, you might believe there must be truth in these thoughts, even if it goes against your inner judgment.

These sorts of feelings can often stem from a fear of the unknown. People can dislike others without truly knowing or understanding much about them.

Society can also tend to promote a competitive spirit, so some people may want to show others that they see themselves as better than them. Disliking those who are different reinforces an individual or group's belief that their way of doing things is the right way.

Hate can also emerge from insecurity or jealousy. If you're feeling threatened or experiencing low self-esteem, it can be easy to simply blame others.

"Hate, it has caused a lot of problems in the world, but has not solved one yet"

Maya Angelou

WHAT IS A HATE CRIME?

This is a criminal offence in which victims are targeted because they belong to a certain group, often because of race, religion, disability, gender identity, or sexual orientation. Hate crimes include intimidation, harassment, threats, or physical attacks.

If you experience, or witness, a hate incident:

* **Report it** Tell a trusted adult such as a teacher, school counselor or nurse, or a family member.

* **Put it in perspective** It doesn't reflect anything you've done but only the other person's prejudice, insecurity, or jealousy. Don't let other people's hatred stop you living life to the fullest.

* **Be active** If you're a member of an under-represented group and feel confident, ask a teacher if you can give a talk or make a display about your religion or disability to dispel stereotypes.

If you experience strong feelings of hatred:

1 Be kind to yourself
Everyone has angry thoughts about others from time to time. These can seem more intense when tired or upset. Go for a walk, rest, or focus on a hobby.

Example: *"I was overwhelmed by feelings of hate and anger toward a sibling and began plotting revenge. After soccer practice and a good night's sleep, I could put it in perspective. I realized I'd been annoyed about an incident at school. A thoughtless comment from my sister had made me target my hate at her."*

2 Realize multiple ways of doing things can all be right
People convince themselves the way they do things must be right and therefore what other people do must be wrong. In reality, there can be many ways of doing things that are all equally valid.

Example: *"I really hated my basketball co-captain who wanted to try out new strategies every game and swap positions all the time. It took me a long time to recognize she had her way of doing things and I had mine. Both were okay, just different."*

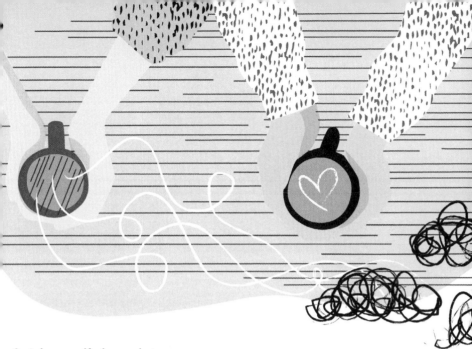

3 Ask yourself why you hate

Sometimes things people hate about others are things they dislike about themselves. Ask yourself what it is about the other person that angers you so much.

Example: *"I wrote in my journal about my feelings toward a group from a different background and I realized I actually liked all the individuals. Other people around me were prejudiced and I was going along with their ideas."*

4 Work on your own identity

Hate can arise from feelings of jealousy, low self-esteem, or inadequacy. Move out of this negative spiral by concentrating on building your own strengths, hobbies, and connections.

Example: *"I hated a group of classmates who seemed to have it all—strong friendships, great social lives, good grades, and lots of talents. So I concentrated on my dancing and my own friends. I found I stopped comparing and didn't mind the other group so much."*

5 Get support

If your feelings are overwhelming or having a negative impact on your life, speak to a school counselor who will help you to cope positively with your emotions.

ARE YOU SEEKING REVENGE... OR JUSTICE?

If someone hurts you, the first reaction is often to want to "get even." Usually, that desire fades. But what if it doesn't? What if you feel you won't rest until you have retaliated? Or are you actually after justice?

The terms revenge and justice are often used together and sometimes confused for one another despite having different meanings. Revenge is an emotional, often knee-jerk, reaction—an angry urge to hit back and cause someone to suffer for the hurt they've caused. Justice, on the other hand, is more concerned with righting a wrong in a way that most people would agree was appropriate. In contrast to revenge, it's about fairness and should correlate with the offence committed.

People might seek revenge when a close friend or relative has been physically harmed, for instance, and lash out in an equally violent manner. But it can also be sought for more day-to-day issues. A mocking comment on a classmate's selfie on Instagram™, for example, can quickly spiral into bullying in the schoolyard.

There are ways to get justice instead of taking revenge: The police can deal with crimes; teachers can deal with school bullies; and your parents can sort out sibling disputes when tussles over who's first into the shower get out of hand.

WHAT IF I WANT REVENGE?

1 **First take a moment to let your feelings out** Write down what's happened and how you feel or speak to a trusted friend who might be able to give you another perspective. It's okay to feel vengeful but you're in control of how you respond. Take the time you need to work out your feelings and explore why you're angry.

2 **Accept your feelings are natural** Everyone wants to retaliate at times. It might help to remind yourself that anger is fueling your thirst for revenge. Try not to let the need to get retribution—or hit back—dominate your thoughts.

3 **Take time to think** You may feel you'll only get satisfaction when you've got revenge—but it will most likely be a temporary relief. You may even be more angry afterward, especially if you've behaved in a way that's out of character.

4 **Consider all the options** Would talking to the person who's upset you be better than seeking revenge? Is there a way to resolve the situation by talking to them and trying to understand why they behaved in an unkind way? Maybe they didn't realize what they were doing or they've made a horrible mistake that they regret.

5 **Do you seek justice?** If you feel that, say, another student or a sibling needs to "pay" for what they've done, who decides the next course of action? If it's at school, it might help to talk to a teacher. At home, you might turn to a trusted family member. Either way, it's safest if they ensure you get justice rather than trying to do it yourself.

6 **Can you move on from the incident?** Speak to a friend, relative, or teacher if you're unsure if it's best not to take any action. Try not to let your mind be consumed by a desire to hurt another person. If justice is possible, get it. If not, try to let it go.

A thoughtful
GIFT

Don't focus on the price tag when you want to mark a friend's birthday or say thank you for a kind gesture. Instead, get creative and think about a different set of values...

1 Care

There are many things you can buy friends, family members, or even teachers as presents, but the reality is you don't need to spend a lot to show someone you care. For most people monetary value is far less important than the thought given to a present. From a framed photograph to a souvenir you bought on a school trip, small, sentimental gifts packed with memories send a powerful message. And the closer you are to a person, the more personal your present can be—it's a real opportunity to prove how well you know them and their interests. Before you make a purchase, think about the personality and taste of the person you're buying for. The trick is to be attentive to what they truly like and observe them properly to discover who they really are, and what they mean to you. It's not the price of the gift that counts, but the thought behind it.

2 Time

You can give your time in so many ways. Homemade presents are unique and show you care enough to make an effort. Creating with passion can also bring a sense of wellbeing and contentment. It could be knitting a scarf with their favorite color yarn, making a greetings card with a self-penned poem inside, or baking delicious cupcakes—whatever you decide, make it special—for them and for you. And a gift doesn't even have to be "something." It could be simply hanging out together, whether it's a night in watching your friend's must-see movie, suggesting you and your mom visit her favorite gallery, or asking a grandparent to tell you more about their childhood (you could even record their recollections). The gift of time is precious—think carefully about how the other person would wish to spend a few hours or a day together.

3 Meaning

Why wait for a birthday or Christmas? From "I'm sorry" to "I love you" and "thank you" to "good luck," gifts can convey many messages and express inner feelings of regret, gratitude, or togetherness when shyness or embarrassment makes the spoken word too difficult. A present can leave the recipient time—and space—to think about the gesture and what it meant. It's a wonderful feeling for the giver, too, as the person will be surprised and touched by such a display of care and attention.

4 Selflessness

There may be times when an anonymous card or present is the ideal way to say thank you or show someone you care about what they are going through. A simple, unsigned "thank you" note for who they are or what they do can have a deep effect and such a selfless act of giving shows true generosity.

PRESENT AND CORRECT

Stuck for ideas? Use these top tips for giving a loved one a special treat…

* **Buy a blank card** This allows you to think about what you really want to say and compose your own message. Use it as a chance to express feelings that you have perhaps never put into words. Be original and honest—you could practice on some scrap paper first to make sure it sounds just right.

* **Present a gift beautifully** Choose gift wrap that reflects their personality or use a ribbon or bow of their favorite color. You could add practical value by placing your gift into a larger "memory box" to which they can add other mementoes later.

* **Arrange a "gift unwrapping" ceremony** Double-wrapping a present or offering two gifts (the first one being a silly or funny object and the second one being the real thing) will make it fun for both of you.

* **Make it special delivery** Leave your gift in a place where it will be found later, perhaps in a coat pocket, a school bag, in a kitchen drawer, or even placed carefully on someone's desk.

"Seek joy in what you give, not in what you get"

Anon

THANKS FOR
EVERYTHING...

When was the last time you said thank you to someone and really
meant it? Noticing and appreciating the good things around you really
can change your life for the better

The great thing about gratitude is that it actually helps you more than the person
you're showing gratitude towards. When you feel thankful and happy with your
own life, you are naturally more grateful and don't feel you want or need as much.
Researchers have proven that "gratitude helps people feel more positive emotions,
enjoy good experiences, improves their health, deals with adversity, and builds
strong relationships." And a study by the University of California even found that
students who score high on gratitude have more friends and do better at school.
So here are some easy ways to show your appreciation…

1 Write on

Put down your tablet, your laptop, your phone… because there's no better way to say thank you to someone than by writing to them. Whoever you are writing to can see the effort you have made and it feels so much more personal than a text or an email. A card, a letter, even a poem, it doesn't need to be perfect.

2 Give it time

Giving your time is a wonderful way to show your gratitude. Suggest watching a movie with someone in your family you haven't taken time to think about recently, or try cooking and eating with friends you haven't seen for a while.

3 Start a family tradition

Make gratitude a habit—suggest you all go around the dinner table saying one thing you're grateful for, noting small things you've enjoyed that day.

4 The gift of giving

Think about the people around you—what could you do to show someone you care? Walk the dog, feed the cat, tidy your room, wash the car, or offer to cook dinner—you'll be surprised how much of a difference these things can make. Think about charitable work that you might be able to do locally—volunteering at a local animal shelter, or helping out in a nursing home. Bake cookies for a friend, or try drawing a picture for a family member.

5 Get in touch

Connect with the people you love by hugging them to say thank you, when you meet them and when you say goodbye. Touch is the first sense we acquire, our first unspoken language, and it is the secret weapon in forming successful relationships.

6 Cheer up a friend

Text or email a picture of something that's inspired your appreciation—a sunset, a silly pet pose, a drawing—to a friend who needs a boost.

7 Keep smiling

And remember, you can make someone's day by simply smiling at them. Whether it's someone serving you in a store, or to provide support and encouragement for a friend—smiling is contagious.

BE A CLIMATE
CRUSADER

Global warming is responsible for major changes in the Earth's climate.
But what can you do to make a difference?

Whether you live in a snowy wilderness or a hot and humid city, the chances are
you'll have started to notice some shifts in the weather, and you may have heard
about more extreme events like hurricanes and droughts on the news. The world's
climate is changing and it's affecting how everyone—the people and animals that
share the planet—will thrive and survive now, and in the future.

Winds of change

Natural disasters, including hurricanes and cyclones, have always been a risk in
some regions of the world, but records show that these extreme weather events
are becoming more frequent and their force greater. Many scientists believe this is
because of climate change.

Climate change describes the difference in regular weather patterns that are
affecting the planet, including changes in temperature and increased occurrences
of floods, wildfires, droughts, hurricanes, and storms.

If the climate changes too fast and too dramatically, humans, animals, plants, and
marine life all suffer, as a result of challenging environmental conditions. Imagine
if where you live suddenly had no water, or if every summer's day was so hot you
couldn't venture outside, or if your island home was in danger of being covered by
rising seas—think how different life might be.

Fueling the flames

Since Earth was formed billions of years ago, it has gone through many different natural cycles of changing temperature and weather. But since the Industrial Revolution, which started in the late 18th century—when humans began burning more fossil fuels, such as oil, coal, and gas, to power their homes, transport, and businesses—the speed with which the globe is warming up has increased.

"We are causing the planet to heat up much faster than it has ever done before," says Aaron Gray-Block, from environmental action group, Greenpeace™. "This is due to the widespread and unprecedented burning of fossil fuels."

When fossil fuels are burned they release carbon into the atmosphere in the form of carbon dioxide (CO_2), which is known as a greenhouse gas because it traps heat from the sun in the atmosphere, which warms up the planet.

Breaking the ice

A temperature increase of even a few degrees not only affects the world's weather systems, but also impacts the vast, ice-covered regions at both the far north and south of the planet. Sitting on the top of the world, the Arctic has been covered by ice for hundreds of thousands—if not millions—of years, but scientists have predicted that the region could be ice-free in the summer months within 30 years.

Meanwhile Antarctica—Earth's southern-most ice-covered continent—has seen an average 41°F temperature rise around its peninsula in the past 60 years. Ancient ice shelves are thinning and icebergs twice the size of Luxembourg are splitting off.

"If we keep polluting our atmosphere with CO_2 and temperatures continue to rise, the world in the future will look very different from what it is today," warns Aaron. "Large areas of our planet and even whole countries will become uninhabitable for humans. Tensions and conflicts will increase as people migrate to find other livable places, water, and food. It will impact animals too, as their habitats will change."

Uncharted waters

Many of Earth's natural wonders have already felt the impact of climate change. In Australia, the world's largest coral reef system, the Great Barrier Reef, has seen large swathes of coral "bleached" by a rise in sea temperature caused by a weather phenomenon called El Niño. This periodic warming isn't new, but climate change is increasing its frequency, meaning the fragile corals—which can only survive in water of 68-89°F—have less time to recover whenever it occurs.

In other parts of the world, low-lying nations like the Maldives and Bangladesh, which sit only just above sea level, could be lost to the ocean forever. Around the world, seas are now rising an average of 0.12 in. per year, and are predicted to climb a total of ½-6½ ft. by 2100.

"There is no time to waste," says Aaron. "We cannot avoid the impacts of climate change. But if we take action to phase out coal as quickly as possible and transition to clean, renewable energy, we will be able to limit them. And while doing so, we will be healing our food production and diets; and providing a better future for our Earth, animals, and us."

"The greatest threat to our planet is the belief that someone else will save it"

Robert Swann

WHAT CAN YOU DO?

Everyone can make a difference when it comes to limiting climate change. Here are a few things you can do to reduce your own "carbon footprint"…

Use less power Switch off lights when you leave the room and take shorter showers—every little helps!

Buy less stuff Do you really need that new top? Every new piece of clothing or gadget you buy is made using power—and much of that power will generate CO2 emissions.

Go green Encourage your family to switch to a green and clean energy provider that uses wind or solar power, rather than coal or gas.

Eat more vegetables The process of farming animals for meat is one of the major contributors of CO2 in the atmosphere. Eating veggies is kinder to the planet (and piggies).

Cut out the car Walk or ride a bicycle whenever you can. Unless they are electric, most cars will be running on fossil fuels.

Speak up Sign and share online petitions asking your local politician or government to help reduce your country's carbon emissions.

Spread the word Think about climate change as a topic for a class project, poem, piece of art, or a school assembly.

Reuse and recycle Ditch single-use plastic bottles, cups, and straws. Not only will it cut down on power (and CO2), it will help the oceans stay plastic-free.

Going from

STRENGTH
TO STRENGTH

Identify your good qualities, then make sure you use them

What do you consider are your strengths? Did you answer that question with a list of things you're good at? Science, history, art, or playing tennis, for example. If so, you're not alone. Most people find it easy to identify the school subjects and hobbies they excel in, but harder to identify their character strengths—the virtues, skills, and aptitudes that can make them feel more energized, motivated, and passionate (check out our list of strengths on page 69).

It's useful to know your strengths. Basing your self-worth just on being "good at math" or "good at swimming" might lead to feelings of insecurity when somebody comes along who is better at math (or swimming), or if illness, injury, or circumstance means you can no longer participate in that activity. In comparison, character strengths are skills you can apply to many different situations and contexts. If you're a good team player, for example, you can put this to use in school, when playing sports, and in your personal and social lives.

Researchers have found that top achievers from many different fields tend to build their lives around their key strengths and then use those qualities to help them overcome the things they find more difficult. People who learn how to work to their strengths are likely to feel more confident and optimistic about what they're doing, and are therefore more likely to achieve their life goals.

COURAGE
PATIENCE
SOCIABILITY
ORIGINALITY
ADAPTABILITY
INTELLIGENCE
GRATITUDE
HONESTY
EMOTIONAL
MODESTY
ENERGY
ENTHUSIASM
LOVE
OPEN-MINDEDNESS
CREATIVITY
GENEROSITY
WISDOM
FORGIVENESS
APPRECIATION OF BEAUTY
INTEGRITY
HOPE
HUMILITY
INDEPENDENCE
KINDNESS
OPTIMISM

IDENTIFYING YOUR STRENGTHS

Some evidence suggests that around one-third of your strengths could be innate (meaning you're born with them), while the other two-thirds are developed over time. That means everyone has the potential to improve various strengths. If you hear yourself saying "I'm not very creative" or "I'm not a patient person," this probably means you haven't yet had the opportunity to develop that particular strength. So, how can you learn to recognize and develop your top qualities?

1 Collect your strengths

At the end of each day, write down three things that have gone well. Add the strengths that you used in those situations. At the end of the week, you'll have a list of strengths you're using on a regular basis.

Example: *"All of my friends were out on a school trip. At lunch I had nobody to talk to. I decided to go to homework club and got ahead with my study."* **Resourcefulness**

"Dad made me my favorite meal as a surprise." **Gratitude**

"I put a lot of effort in while at trampoline club and have offered to help the younger students next week." **Enthusiasm**

2 Cultivate your strengths

Seek out opportunities to use and develop your strengths in new ways. This will help you to gain new skills, as well as enhancing your existing strengths. Write these down.

Example: *"I enjoy being creative, so I'm going to try out the local craft club."*

"I've a real love of learning. Next time I go to the library, I'll take out some books on two new nonfiction topics."

> "It's important to remember that we all have magic inside of us"
>
> J.K. Rowling

3 Reframe any less positive comments

If you've received comments that you perceive as negative, don't worry. Try reframing the opinion to find some of your hidden strengths.

Example: *"A classmate said I'm weird, but I know I'm original and true to myself."*

"I've been told I'm not good at group work, but this just shows my strength is in working independently."

4 Use top strengths to develop lesser strengths

If you'd like to develop one of your lesser strengths further, try using a top strength to help you along the way.

Example: *"I'd say patience is one of my lesser strengths as I become very frustrated waiting around with nothing to do. But planning and organization are two of my top strengths. Next time I think I might have a wait ahead of me, I'll be organized and take a book or magazine with me."*

"I find it hard to forgive others. One of my strengths is creativity, so I could try to express and work through my feelings by painting or writing a short story."

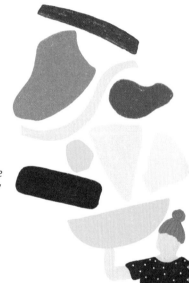

Consider your strengths by completing these sentences:

* Others have told me I'm…
* Strengths I've used this week are…
* I could use my top strengths more by…

WHICH ARE YOUR CHARACTER STRENGTHS?

Use this list to check off any you think form part of your personality…

- ADAPTABILITY
- APPRECIATION OF BEAUTY
- AUTHENTICITY
- CONSCIENTIOUSNESS
- COURAGE
- CREATIVITY
- CRITICAL THINKING
- EMOTIONAL INTELLIGENCE
- ENERGY
- ENTHUSIASM
- FAIRNESS
- FORGIVENESS
- GENEROSITY
- GRATITUDE
- HONESTY
- HOPE
- HUMILITY
- HUMOR
- INDEPENDENCE
- INTEGRITY

- KINDNESS
- LEADERSHIP
- LOGICAL THINKING
- LOVE OF LEARNING
- LOVE
- MODESTY
- OPEN-MINDEDNESS
- OPTIMISM
- ORGANIZATION
- ORIGINALITY
- PATIENCE
- PERSEVERANCE
- RELIABILITY
- RESPONSIBILITY
- SELF-AWARENESS
- SELF-CONTROL
- SOCIABILITY
- SPIRITUALITY
- TEAMWORK
- WISDOM

MODESTY

START BELIEVING...

...and stop putting yourself down. If you refuse
to listen to your inner doubts and try even when
you know you might fail, you give yourself the
chance to fulfill your potential

Beating yourself up with negative thoughts and feelings can get in the way of reaching what you really want. It's called self-sabotage. There are lots of ways you might be doing it. You might think too much—or put off doing things. You plan to act, but get lost when you have to make a decision, and drag your heels. You may turn down trying something new even though deep down you think it could be fun, or refuse to finish homework, when actually you'd love to get good grades.

So, how do you know your inner saboteur is at work?
One tell-tale sign is that when there's something you know you want, for some reason you seem to do everything in your power to make sure you don't get it. As strange as it may sound, the reason you self-sabotage is to protect yourself. If you don't put yourself into a position where you might fail, you won't experience the thing you fear might happen. But on the flip side, you also won't achieve what you really want.

The reason for self-sabotage is fear, one of your natural survival instincts. When you put yourself in a situation that you know you might find difficult, you risk rejection or failure. It is this fear that is guiding your thoughts. It is fear that's holding you back.

Here are some other signs that fear of failure might be holding you back:

* Failing makes you worry about what others are thinking about you

* Failing makes you worry that you're not that clever or good at things

* Failing makes you worry about letting down family or friends you care about

* Before you do something you tell people you probably won't be good at it to lower their expectations

* When there's something you need to prepare for—maybe a test or a speech you need to give at school—you get distracted by tasks that with hindsight probably weren't that urgent

* Before a big event you always seem to "run out of time" to properly prepare, or suffer with last-minute aches and pains that interfere with you being ready

Time to face your fears

Unless you face your anxieties, you risk letting your inner saboteur stand in the way of your successes. But to do this, you have to step out of your familiar comfort zone and try something different, which is harder than it sounds.

You see, there's a part of the brain that doesn't like change, registering it as unfamiliar, risky, and unsafe. It tries to stop you in your tracks by building up resistance—telling you all the reasons you shouldn't do it.

Think of it as though you were skydiving. As you're about to jump out of the plane your brain senses a threat to your survival. It reacts by building up resistance as it tries to stop you from making the leap in order to keep you safe. If you want to stop fear holding you back, you have to push through this resistance and find the courage to jump, so that you can spread your wings and fulfill your true potential.

"The most certain way to succeed is always to try just one more time"

Thomas A. Edison

LET GO OF NEGATIVE THOUGHTS

Sometimes physical actions can help to release feelings you'd like to let go of. Next time you notice a negative thought, try this exercise…

Find something to write with that can easily be erased or washed away. This could be a pencil on paper, a piece of chalk on a blackboard, a washable pen on a tile or mirror (make sure it isn't permanent!), or even a paintbrush dipped in water to use on a stone.

Take the pencil, pen, or brush and draw, write, or doodle whatever thoughts you want to release.

Now take a cloth or eraser and wipe those thoughts away. Notice how the words disappear. Sometimes it may take a little scrubbing to get all of them, but watch the thoughts being washed away along with any bad feelings you've picked up over the day.

BY POPULAR DEMAND

Not everyone is as cool and clever as they would like you to believe. So start having faith in the person who matters most—you

Do you ever look at people and wish you were like them? There are students at every school who are labeled as "cool." They're popular and everyone wants to be their friend. All their Instagram™ posts seem to have lots of likes, and they always seem to be going out, wearing fashionable clothes, and doing amazing things.

In comparison, you may feel you don't fit in or have many friends. You may dream of being that popular person or part of the cool gang whose selfies are complimented by thousands and who attend every party happening. It's easy to start questioning why you aren't "liked" as much, which is why on the next page there are some tips to help you realize that being popular isn't as important as it seems…

TOO COOL FOR SCHOOL

1 No one is perfect

It's easy to watch the cool kids and think they have it all, but appearances can be deceptive. While their social media posts and personality may suggest happiness all around, most people struggle with something in their life, whether it's a family problem, health issue, or emotional trouble. Many are just good at hiding it. Try to be happy with what you have and realize everyone is unhappy about something. It can help to change your outlook on life.

2 Comparing yourself to others will make you sad

You are one of a kind... unique, wonderful you. You may not be the top of the class in every subject, have the hair color, teeth, skin, or body like someone you admire, or have hundreds of friends, but you're an amazing human being who makes a difference to many people's lives. If you compare yourself to others, you waste time and energy and can become unhappy and resentful. Start focusing on the one life you can control—yours. You can't always change how others think, but you can change your thoughts.

3 Accept your differences

Accept who you are and how brilliant you are. Look around at all the people at your school and you'll see they're all different in how they look and act. Instead of comparing yourself to any of them, focus on all the good things about yourself. Ask someone you trust what your best characteristics are and be proud of these. Few people receive regular compliments so it'll be weird to listen to, but also nice—and when you realize this and feel a glow inside, it could spur you on to give a compliment to someone else who may need a boost.

4 What is popularity anyway?

Take time to think what it is about the popular people that you like. Do you really agree with their views and what they stand for? Would you change your hobbies and lifestyle to be like them? Or do you simply want to have that feeling of being popular to feel validated? Popularity isn't everything. If you're a good, kind, and honest person, who cares about reaching their goals, that should go a long way to helping you succeed in life. Popularity doesn't guarantee anything.

5 Quality not quantity

You may worry that you have few friends compared to some people, but don't judge yourself by a number. One or two good, solid friendships mean far more than lots of fleeting ones. Quite often, those with hundreds of friends don't have many close relationships. They have people to go out with but no one to open up to. Take time to value people you really care about, who won't talk about you behind your back. Aim to enjoy the friendships you have.

6 Focus on the most important person—you!

If you're going to compare yourself to anyone, then compare yourself to you. Everyone can try to be a better version of themselves, whether it's improving artistic skills, developing fitness, or growing as a person. Celebrate the improvements you make in your life each week and be proud of your achievements and how far you've come.

7 Deal with your insecurities

If you really struggle with the fact you're not as popular as you would like, seek help to improve your self-image and confidence. Speak to a parent or teacher about how you feel. Many adults will tell you that feeling unpopular or as though you don't fit in is part of life—it's just something few people admit. The older you get, the more people you'll meet from different walks of life, and suddenly popularity won't matter any more. One day you'll look back and wish you hadn't wasted so much time and energy comparing yourself to others when you were a fantastic person just as you were.

BEST

SELF - WORTH

anxiety

SELF - ESTEEM

vulnerability

criticism

your BEST really is ENOUGH

SELF - DOUBT

I'm a HAPPY KIND + THOUGHTFUL human being

failure

YOUR BEST IS ENOUGH

While being the school overachiever may seem an enviable role, it does have its downsides. After all, what happens when you lose the No. 1 spot? Learning how to face this and move on can be tricky

Throughout life, there's pressure from society to be the best at whatever you do. It could be a test at school, a dance competition, a sports game, or even how many likes your photos get on Instagram™.

Most people are happy knowing they've done the best they can and, because they rarely come top, learn to deal with that feeling. But what if you're an overachiever and constantly feel the pressure of being the absolute best?

What is an "overachiever"?
Overachievers seem to excel at everything. They do well in tests, produce amazing homework week after week, are top scorers in what seems like every sport they try, and are often involved in lots of organizations and events outside of school and at the weekends. Their fellow students or colleagues are left wondering how they fit it all in.

But being a top performer has its downsides. Some overachievers link their successes to their self-worth and worry how people will see them when they make mistakes or don't come top of the class, which they perceive as failure. As a result, their self-esteem is dented and they can experience painful self-doubt about their value as a person. Most will hide these worries, fearful that if they show vulnerability their peers will judge them to have failed.

This constant fear of not being the best or getting something wrong means overachievers can easily become stressed and anxious. They'll do everything they can to avoid not being perfect and this can have a negative impact on their mental health. So, if this sounds like you or a friend, what can you do to help?

BELIEVE IN YOURSELF

1 Embrace failure

The most important remedy to this anxiety is to learn how to fail and move on. It might be that you're not the winner or perfect at times, but accept you worked hard and did your best. Failure sounds like a negative word but think of it as a learning experience. No one is the best all the time. You are human. Some of the world's most accomplished people failed many times before achieving their goals.

J.K. Rowling, author of the *Harry Potter* series, experienced huge hardships before finding success; legendary film-maker Walt Disney was fired from one of his first jobs as a cartoonist because he didn't have many ideas; and Michael Jordan, who was ditched from his basketball team, went on to become one of the sport's most successful players ever.

Alongside failure, criticism is an overachiever's nightmare. No one likes to be told their work isn't perfect, but to someone who consistently excels, it can be brutal. One way to overcome this is to learn to listen to criticism without it affecting your self-esteem. It may be constructive and help you to improve an element of coursework, for instance. There will also be negative comments that are unpleasant and unjustified. It can be difficult, but ignore this type of criticism as best you can.

"We are all failures—at least the best of us are"

J.M. Barrie

2 It's all about you

Don't feel the only thing that makes you a good person is being the best. First, there is more to a person than grades, awards, and packing your life to the brim with clubs and organizations. What's more important is being happy and a kind, thoughtful, decent human being. No one can be good at everything. Would you look down on a student who got a lower grade in an exam even though they'd worked hard?

With the best will in the world, you can't always change what others do, think, or say, but you can decide how you react and deal with people and their expectations. And if friends do think less of you for not doing something as well as you promised… well, they're not great friends.

3 Accept that your best is enough

It's important to realize not everyone will always be the winner. Look at athletes who are at the top of their game, such as gymnast Simone Biles. They don't win all the time—but they do learn from their disappointments. What sets high performers aside from overachievers is that they are content knowing they do the best they can do and are proud of any progress they make. So next time something doesn't go as you wanted it, remember: Your best really is enough.

SENSE AND
SENSITIVITY

Far from being weak and fragile, softer souls have a hidden strength

Accept who you are

Do you struggle not to cry if someone raises a voice at you? Do seemingly small things reduce you to tears? Being tense and touchy are some of the traits of a sensitive person—someone who rather than being insecure just perceives the world differently. They feel deeply and can be weighed down by the experience, sometimes overwhelmed and paralyzed by intense emotions, be they anger, love, or sadness. If this sounds like you (take the sensitivity test over the page), try not to resent this part of yourself and instead accept it as an asset that makes you more perceptive and intuitive.

A gift in disguise

You can turn what you may consider a weakness into strength. You're lucky enough to have this special ability—being able to feel and see things that others may not—so you could use it for your and others' benefit. Like many things in life, you have the power to develop what some regard as a disadvantage into a positive inner force. So, try not to dismiss it or see it as a burden. Perhaps consider it a gift and an opportunity to grow and learn. By having a greater sensory perception, you can sense the nuances of beauty, especially in arts or nature, but also in all the little things that make life wonderful. It's important to remember these instances given that your ability means you will feel life's injustices just as sharply.

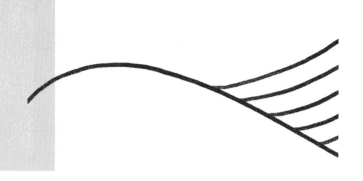

Cherish the difference

Some people think it's better to disguise your feelings or pretend you don't have them. But why? Showing your feelings—good or bad—is not a curse. Feeling deeply is an asset that allows you to be aware of your surroundings, be tuned into other people's concerns, and to enjoy life's sweet experiences to the fullest. There's no reason to be ashamed because you're sensitive, so try not to make yourself emotionally numb so you can look tough in front of others. This isn't who you are and while hiding your emotions may seem to be a useful coping mechanism at first, it might make it harder when they all inevitably come flooding back in.

Enhance your relationships

Your openness to the world allows you to interact better with others: You can easily interpret people's emotions and understand their pain. Being able to empathize with someone is a genuine gift—try to cherish it. And it might be that your ability to show your own feelings will have a positive effect on those around you. A scientific phenomenon known as "emotional contagion" suggests that your emotions actually rub off on others, so like a ripple effect, when you show happiness you also raise the mood of the people close to you.

See sensitivity as a strength

Still, you carry the weight of the world on your shoulders, you feel the pain of others and you give them everything you have. Being sensitive is hard… but if you embrace your sensitive nature to the fullest, you can appreciate the many benefits it offers in everyday life, from noticing everything to being able to comfort others, from feeling more intensely to truly caring. You may have been called overdramatic or soft, but the problem is not you—it's part of societies where emotions have been switched off. Don't think you have to change to fit in, instead nurture this because being a sensitive soul is a sign of strength—not a weakness.

ARE YOU A SENSITIVE PERSON?

* Have difficulty letting go of negative thoughts and emotions?

* Worry about what others think?

* Struggle to accept critical feedback?

* Take things personally?

* Detail oriented and think deeply?

* Love—and hate—passionately?

* Cry when watching sad (and sometimes even happy) movies?

* Get upset if you make a bad decision?

* Hate loud noises and bright lights or feel uncomfortable in crowds?

* Feel under pressure when observed doing a task?

The more questions to which you've answered yes, the greater the likelihood that you have the gift of sense and sensitivity.

"When we feel deeply, we reason profoundly"

Mary Wollstonecraft

LIAR, LIAR...

The truth, the whole truth, and nothing but the truth—or is it?

It's not easy to tell the whole truth all of the time. There are occasions when you might feel the need to lie because you don't want to disappoint or upset someone you care about. Think about when a friend's shopping for clothes. If they ask your opinion about, say, an awful jacket they think makes them look amazing, telling the truth—that you think it doesn't suit them—could be hurtful. Sometimes it seems easier to lie and say: "Yeah, you look great." But while such small or "white" lies might seem kind, they can affect other people's trust in you. If your friend buys the jacket only to be mocked in the schoolyard, what will they think of you then? Other options might have been: "I'm not sure" or "I think the sleeves are a bit short." If your friend had decided she loved the jacket then—and now—then good for her. And you would feel happier that you hadn't lied.

THE TRUTH ABOUT LIES

1 Bigging yourself up
Sometimes you might find yourself telling white lies in an attempt to fit in with others. Most people exaggerate now and again to impress people, whether it's about how amazing their weekend was or how many friends they have. You might also be tempted to lie to cover your tracks. If a teacher asks you why you're late handing in homework, for example, you might respond: "My laptop is broken," rather than, "I was watching YouTube™ videos."

2 Bad reputation

Try to remember that getting known for telling lies, even if they're only small ones, can land you in trouble and ruin close relationships. There's a saying that if you tell one lie, you end up telling a thousand and that's because you have to keep covering up the lie every time someone questions you. It can become impossible to remember what you've said and it means you can start believing your own lies.

3 Breaking the trust

In all relationships, whether it's with family, close friends, or schoolmates, it's important to know how to build up trust. What seems a small or white lie to one person can be perceived as a deliberate attempt to mislead or betray by someone else. Telling your best friend you stayed in last night when you met another friend might seem harmless enough. But if your best friend hears about it from someone else, they'll probably feel upset that you weren't honest with them and question your friendship.

4 Understand the consequences

Be aware that not owning up to a small thing you've done wrong might mean that someone else gets the blame. And once people find out you've not told the truth, they'll be less likely to believe what you say in the future.

5 The truth can hurt

People often tell lies because they don't like awkward situations or want to avoid a confrontation. But as British poet John Lydgate said: "You can please some of the people all of the time, all of the people some of the time, but you can never please all of the people all of the time." In other words, you have to risk hurting other people's feelings now and again so that you can stay truthful.

6 Break the habit

Lying can be habit forming and so the first step is to break the habit. There are ways to explain yourself and your actions honestly, without lying or undermining your own truth. Try to identify the situations, emotions, places, or people that tend to cause you to avoid telling the truth. It might be that you lie when you're anxious about doing well at school or you lie to particular people who you may feel a little scared of. Once you recognize what "triggers" your lies, you can either avoid the trigger or find a way to face it with honesty. Take a deep breath, choose your words carefully, and feel confident in the fact that you are being truthful. It can take getting used to, but people will respect you for your honesty in the long run.

How to tame
NEGATIVE
THOUGHTS

Sometimes the stress of friendship circles, school exams, and social media can lead to gloomy thoughts and negative thinking. Everyone has their own unique triggers, but once the worries start, they can be hard to switch off. If you can't stop them, imagine how it would feel if you could tame them, and use them to make your life better instead

Negative thoughts can come from anything—events that really happened or hopes and fears about the future. They might be judgmental of the outside world ("this movie is so lame"), or of yourself ("I'm such a dope"), and can be much meaner than you would ever be out loud. Many happen almost unconsciously, so these thought patterns build up over time. When you think: "I'm so stressed out," it creates a stress response in the body, as if following orders. And when you're in this mode, everything seems a threat, creating more negative thoughts. This creates a vicious circle—mind to body, body to mind.

Living like this can leave you feeling overwhelmed and anxious. It can also have physical health consequences because the body isn't as good at digestion and healing in this state. Health problems from stress include swings in weight and mood, digestion problems, and tightness and pain in the back, neck, and shoulders.

From mind to body

One way to get out of a negative thought pattern is to get into the body—to focus on the way that you feel. This has a few effects. First, it takes you away from thinking about the past or future, and brings you into the present. Secondly, feelings are messages. Giving yourself permission to feel is a powerful way of listening to your own truth and intuition. Use them to help you understand what you're drawn toward or away from.

Being honest about your feelings might be challenging. Noticing someone or something that makes you feel awful can mean having to make difficult choices. When you're honest with yourself, you can begin to address your own wishes.

Choose to see things differently

Moving away from negative thinking means making powerful choices about the thoughts you want to focus on. Instead of seeing things through a lens of success or failure, smart or dumb, good or bad, concentrate on learning, growing, getting stronger, or more resilient. Everyone says stupid things to the wrong person, or gets things wrong. Next time you start to criticize yourself, especially thinking you are a particular thing (stupid, lazy, or whatever), shift that into something to develop (new study skills or habits).

Focus on the thoughts you want to have

Another change is to envision the thoughts and feelings that you want. Some thoughts, like worry, set you up for stress. If an exam fills you with anxiety, instead of thinking: "I'm going to fail, and then my life is over," you can think about how you want to feel during the exam. "During my math exam, I will feel clearheaded, so I can remember the formulas I need to do the work." That can become an affirmation or mantra, something you mentally repeat to yourself on a regular basis, which sets you up to feel different in the moment.

Your negative thoughts are not your enemy. Become curious about them. Imagine your negative thought is your body's way of trying to keep you safe. What is it keeping you safe from? Is that something you need to be protected from, or a fear you can let go? Ask yourself these questions regularly and, over time, you'll come to see your thoughts in a new light.

Everyone goes through periods of feeling down or stressed, but if these patterns persist for two weeks or more it may be a sign that there's something more serious going on. If this happens, try talking to a trusted adult such as a family member, doctor, teacher, school counselor, or nurse.

A TRANSFORMATION CHALLENGE

*Try to do this at least once a day, for seven days, when you
notice a nasty thought directed toward yourself:*

Notice the thought

* Take a deep breath (you can put a hand on your own chest
  if it feels good)

* Ask yourself what feeling lies beneath the thought (is it fear,
  insecurity, love, or sadness?)

* Now ask yourself what you could change or learn to do better
  to meet that feeling (perhaps studying more, finding a new
  friendship group, joining a new club, or speaking to a trusted
  person about your situation)

* Write it down

* Take another deep breath

* Congratulate yourself for listening to you

Ways to get out of the mind and into the body

* **Exercise** Walking, running, or swimming can get you in a zone,
  and yoga can help with mind/body focus

* **Take deep breaths** It might help to put your hands on your ribs
  and feel them move as you breathe

* **Spend time with people who lift you up** Put effort into friendships
  with supportive people who make you feel good about yourself

IT'S OKAY TO CRY

Have you ever felt like you've had to hold back tears because you think they're a sign of weakness? Discover why letting them flow can actually be healthy and good for you

Why people cry
Emotional tears, which are sometimes called "psychic tears," are a way of expressing yourself without talking. Lots of people cry emotional tears. People cry because they're sad, hurt, upset, angry, frustrated, grieving, or in pain. Some cry tears of joy and relief, while others weep after watching a sad movie. Tears can be shed as a result of stress, changes in your body, or simply through having an off-day, and sometimes people just feel like they need to cry without any obvious reason to do so. The bottom line? Whatever your reason for a good sob, it's all okay.

Crying is natural
You make tears to keep eyes healthy—free of annoying dust and dirt—as well as an emotional response. It's totally natural and healthy to cry and is part of how the body copes. So, although it might feel like a sign of weakness and make you feel a little embarrassed, especially to be caught crying in front of family, friends, or people you don't know, it shows that you're emotionally connected. It actually takes real inner strength to be able to express your feelings in such a way.

Although no one really likes to cry or see people they love in tears, especially for sad or painful reasons, it offers an emotional release and people often feel a lot better when they've had a good old weep.

LET THE TEARS FALL

How to cry

Everyone's different. Some people will cry openly and others will do so behind closed doors. Some people are reduced to tears at what might seem to be the smallest thing. Other people, who have gone through some of the most challenging times, might not be able to express themselves in the same way.

There are no rules on how or when to cry. You have to go with how you feel in the moment. The main thing is not to bottle up your emotions. Let those tears flow as and when you need to, and don't feel embarrassed or worry about what others think. Cry if you want to.

Tears of joy

Have you ever thought it strange that people cry tears of joy? Scientists have recently discovered that tears are actually an appropriate response. Their studies show that crying is most likely the body's way of restoring balance when someone is dealing with an intense emotion. People who are overwhelmed by positive news react with tears, allowing them to recover from intense emotions. A person overjoyed at being reunited with a partner returning from war might cry tears of joy, for example.

And the opposite can also be true. Strong negative feelings may provoke positive expressions. People might laugh, for example, when they find themselves in a difficult or frightening situation, while very sad people sometimes smile.

Beware false tears

Some people pretend to cry or use their tears to either get sympathy, attention, or to take advantage of someone else. This is often referred to as false or crocodile tears, and is a display of emotion that isn't real.

"Tears come from the heart
and not from the brain"

Leonardo da Vinci

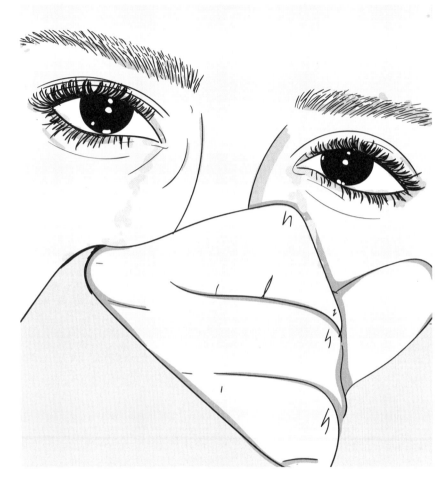

Can't stop crying?

If you feel that you're crying too much, particularly over small things that don't normally bother you, or you're shedding tears often without any apparent reason, this could be a sign that you're under stress. Anxiety, depression, worry, tension, and any emotional problems yet to be sorted out can cause spells of weeping.

If you feel that there's something else going on deep down, it might be an idea to have an honest talk with an adult you feel comfortable with. Crying helps, but sometimes you just need a bit of loving advice to work out how you're feeling.

REASONS WHY IT'S GOOD TO CRY

1 Helps to process emotions
Rather than storing up those difficult feelings or pretending everything's fine when it isn't, a good cry can help you let go of that upsetting energy. Once those tears are released, you can often see something much clearer. It's a great way of working through thoughts and feelings and letting go of whatever isn't supporting you.

2 Releases stress
If you're feeling overwhelmed and feel like crying, then let those tears flow. It's like letting the air out of a balloon—a release that can reduce stress and calm your nervous system. Afterward, you'll be more relaxed.

3 Keeps your emotional balance
When left to build up, feelings can easily grow intense and cause extreme sensations, responses, or behavior that can create more hurt and upset for yourself and other people. Rather than let emotions get out of control, it might be a good idea to let yourself cry instead.

4 It's comforting
When it all feels too much, having a good weep can help you and will make everything seem better.

5 It's a sign you care
If you find yourself crying out of a deep feeling for others or when watching local or world events, you're probably a caring and compassionate person with deep emotions. See this as a positive.

6 Tears keep you healthy
When you cry, your tears also help to wash out germs and annoying bits of dust and dirt.

DON'T MIND REGRETS

Looking back at a situation and wishing you'd done, or said, something differently is natural—it's a part of life's journey. It's what you do with those regrets that makes the difference...

What is regret?

If you find yourself wishing you could travel back in time to change a particular outcome, you're experiencing regret. Angst, guilt, embarrassment, shame, loss, and sadness are the feelings that commonly arise from having regrets and, if left unresolved, can have a big impact on how you live your life. Everyone wants to be able to live without having regrets, of course, but life doesn't always work out that way. Most people, if they're honest, will have some regrets.

The causes of regret

* Speaking without thinking first and then suddenly realizing that you've said something hurtful.

* Failing to say something, such as not speaking up for yourself or others, or missing the opportunity to tell someone that you really care about them.

* Making what seems like the wrong decision, leading to thoughts such as *"If only I'd made a different choice"*.

* Failing to take action when it was needed, such as: *"If I'd spent more time studying, I'd have had a better chance of passing the test"* or *"If I'd got there when I said I would, we'd probably still be friends"*.

* Taking any action, whether deliberate or unintended, that leads to unwanted outcomes.

TYPES OF REGRET

There are essentially two types of regret—productive and unproductive:

1. A **productive** regret is one that can be classed as experience. Perhaps it's a missed opportunity or making a choice that doesn't work out. You might be upset or annoyed for a short time, but it's something you can easily put behind you and even learn from. This kind of regret doesn't usually stop you from taking action in the future.
2. An **unproductive** regret is one that works against you. Maybe you said something embarrassing and are now too shy to speak out in public. It might be that you find yourself replaying the scenario over and over in your head. This kind of regret can freeze you from taking action and can hold you back from living a full life.

It's quite common to experience productive and unproductive regrets as you go through life. As frustrating and difficult as unproductive regret can be, remember that you can still turn this around—it can provide you with some of life's greatest and most valuable lessons that will, with attention, help you to grow.

What you can learn from regret

If you're struggling with unproductive regret and feel it's having a negative impact on your life, consider the following:

* Accept what happened, happened. Can you make amends? If not, think about what you can learn from the experience and how you can do better next time.

* What emotions are at the root of your regret? Acknowledge them and then be prepared to let them go.

* Forgive yourself. Everyone makes mistakes and less-than-wise choices. You won't be the first or only person who's ever done something without thinking.

* Rather than agonize about what you can't change, focus on areas where you can have an impact. Consider how you can make fresh opportunities.

PREVENTING REGRETTABLE OUTCOMES

There will always be situations that cause regret, but you can ward off most of these by being mindful about what you say and do…

1 To avoid making comments you might regret, pause for a moment before saying anything at all. Ask yourself if your words will be helpful, supportive, kind, truthful, or necessary. Is there a better way of getting across what you feel needs to be said? Silence is golden, but there will be times when you need to speak out. Choose your words wisely. Try to avoid speaking from a place of anger or heightened emotions. Bear in mind that even with the most carefully chosen words and the right situation in which to use them, some people might still react in an unintended or unexpected way.

2 To avoid taking action on something you might regret, consider the possible outcomes of your approach. Research, plan, and consider why you want to do what you want to. In some situations, there may not be time to consider all your options and a quick, on-the-spot choice has to be made. All you can do in these circumstances is take action on what feels right. Even if things don't turn out the way you wanted, accept that you did your best.

CREATE A SELF-CARE KIT

In need of a little pampering? Everyone likes to feel good, but when life's busy you can easily overlook the importance of giving yourself some tender loving care. By having your own self-care kit, filled with items that nurture, inspire, and uplift you, you're taking responsibility for your happiness and well-being. You'll have instant access to a special kit that will brighten your spirit, even on the most challenging of days. It's like a big hug to yourself to help you destress and restore your emotional harmony.

HOW TO MAKE YOUR KIT

Use a wicker basket, cardboard shoe box, empty jar, dedicated drawer, or drawstring bag for your self-care kit. This is an opportunity to get creative. Add your own personal touches by decorating the kit to suit your style and personality.

Think about what you can put in your self-care kit. What lights you up and makes you feel amazing? What always puts a big grin on your face when you least feel like smiling? What never fails to comfort and nourish you?

Choose healthy, nonfood treats to go in your kit, items that will nurture, pamper, inspire, motivate, and encourage you. Include the things that are most likely to appeal to your senses, so that you can get out of your overthinking head and into your feelings and imagination.

It doesn't need to cost much to fill your kit. Look out for free samples or trial-size items. You probably already have a few things, something old or something new, that you can put in your kit right now. Remember to keep replenishing your kit with awesome goodies.

Find time for yourself

Keep your self-care kit on-hand and make it your go-to whenever you feel the need for a pick-me-up. Gift yourself the time and space you need to explore the items in your kit, and choose what you feel is needed in that particular moment. Whatever you choose, embrace it. Be kind to yourself. Enjoy this self-nurturing time without expectations or criticism. More often than not, just allowing yourself this breathing space will naturally contribute toward you feeling more relaxed, peaceful, and quietly invigorated.

FEEL-GOOD GOODIES

1 A beautiful notebook and pen
Write or doodle. Fill your notebook with whatever you wish to express in words or pictures. It doesn't have to be pretty or perfect. Aim to finish with a few good words or a picture that will make you smile and feel at ease.

2 Meditation audio
Alison Sellers is a Relax Kids Coach from the UK who helps young people to find their inner calm and be their best self. She says: "An audio meditation that cultivates self-compassion can be very uplifting, especially when you focus on the mantra 'Breathe in happiness, breathe out a smile.'" Just by smiling, it boosts your mood and can trick your brain to release happy hormones so that you feel good instantly.

3 Mini-spa set
Include a few bodycare items in your kit, such as a small bottle of aromatic bubble bath, foot lotion, skin moisturizer, or hand cream with wonderful fragrances to tantalize your senses. Treat yourself and relax.

4 Tea
Include a selection of delicious teas, such as lemon and ginger, blackcurrant and blueberry, mint and lemon, or strawberry and vanilla. Take some time to treat yourself to a reviving tea, indulging your senses in the taste and aroma. Sit still for a while, sip your tea, and let your mind be free for a moment—enjoy a daydream.

5 Inspirational quotes
Dr. Andrea Pennington, international best-selling author of *I Love You, Me!*, suggests: "On a day you're feeling great, make some cute little colorful cards with inspirational quotes, which

you'll be happy to read later. You can also write inspiring messages to yourself about what you love about you, and what makes YOU unique and special."

6 Love notes

Ask a few close friends to write about your three best qualities. You can then read these notes whenever you need a reminder that you are loved and appreciated.

7 Feel-good pictures

Include in your kit a selection of the photos or postcards that are meaningful to you—ones that make you smile or you find inspiring. These can be photos that evoke happy memories of good times with family and friends or shots of places you've visited or have yet to explore.

8 Music and movies

What are your favorite feel-good songs and movies? Add a couple of them to your kit. For an instant pick-me-up, listen to one of those songs. Or if you have more time to spare, watch the movie. Then let all your cares drift away.

9 A favorite verse

Do you have a favorite poem that is light of heart? Write it out and add it to your self-care kit. You can then recite it whenever you need to hear those uplifting words. There's lots of poetry inspiration at poetryfoundation.org.

10 Extra essentials

Of course every kit should include a new pair of soft-touch socks, a luscious lip balm, a paperback novel, a lucky charm, exotic perfume, and something that reminds you of just how amazing you are.

Take a breath and
LOOK OUTSIDE

Can't stop worrying or thinking about something? Find a
window with a view and try this exercise

Stand or sit comfortably and look outside. What can you see? Trees,
a road, the sky? Look left, look right, then up and down, so that you
can see everything in your view.

**Notice the colors, the textures, any patterns. Be aware of how many
different shapes you can see just in this tiny window on the world.**

Pay attention to the space above the horizon, and take a deep breath.
Look out past the horizon and up to the sky.

**Is there anything moving? Find the fastest moving object in your
vision. Now find the slowest. Be aware that they are moving,
and that you are still.**

Choose a natural object and focus on watching it for a moment or two.
This could be a plant or a bird, or even the clouds.

**Look at it as if you are seeing it for the first time. Notice its shape,
its weight, where it touches surrounding objects. Focus on the finer,
intricate details.**

Don't do anything except notice the thing you are looking at. Just
relax into watching it for as long as your concentration allows.

**Take a deep breath in and out. You're ready to carry on
with your day.**

"WELL, AREN'T YOU THE PERFECT ONE..."

Brothers and sisters can be great, but there are also times when they're tiresome, especially if they cast a seemingly splendid shadow and you're the one living in it

Having a brother or sister to share everyday adventures with can be one of the best feelings in the world. Whether it's playing games at home, listening to music together, or joking about dad's cooking, they're always around and usually happy to join in new experiences.

But not all sibling relationships are harmonious. Many, if not most, are characterized by a certain level of rivalry. Seemingly trivial activities, such as who sits where for dinner or who uses the shower first in the morning, can morph into the most ferocious of combat zones.

At times, every little decision can feel like a huge battle and prompt cries of: "Why does she always get her own way?" or "Why doesn't he ever listen to me?"

This is common, pretty much expected, and chances are each sibling will feel that they're treated unfairly in the family setup.

Competitive element

The rivalry can start at any age. Often it begins when a newborn arrives, bringing with it competition for parental attention and upsetting the balance of power in the home. It can also occur later on when academic achievements or extracurricular successes exacerbate underlying tensions and trigger negative emotions. If a sibling excels at singing or dancing, for example, and constantly talks about their successes with friends and family, it could leave you feeling overshadowed. This can be made worse if your parents also seem to be overly proud of a sibling's achievements.

In these circumstances, experiencing resentment, jealousy, frustration, and anger is natural and in the heat of the moment you may even tell your sibling you don't like them any more.

Possessions are often another cause of disputes. Shared access to a computer, TV, tablet, or MP3 player will often be perceived as unequal by one if not both parties. It always seems like you never get your fair amount of time on them.

Parents or friends can also add to the tension, especially if it appears they're more interested in your sibling than they are you or they make unhelpful comparisons. "Why can't you be more like your brother?" or "I don't know what happened with you, your sister's so good at math…" are irritating, hurtful, and unhelpful statements. Thankfully, these feelings fade over time and the most volatile of siblings often grow up to be the best of friends.

But living under the same roof with a sibling can be tough and if you're going through a difficult time right now and tired of the endless fighting, what can you do today to make your situation better? Talking will help, but this can be fraught, so turn the page for a few pointers to get you started.

"Always try to be a little kinder than is necessary"

J.M. Barrie

WAYS TO TALK IT THROUGH

* If you think you can, go directly to the source of the conflict and calmly and politely let your sibling know exactly how you're feeling.

* Timing is key. It's best not to approach them after a heated argument about who used the last of the shampoo. Be cool and try not to be judgmental. Asking: "Why do you think you're so much better than me?" probably isn't the best opening line—and remember there's a chance your own behavior might have been less than helpful.

* It's better to be honest, receptive to their feelings (while not forgetting your own), and to get everything out into the open. Try telling them you don't want to fight any more. There's a good chance they'll be relieved you've taken the first step to helping you both create a more amicable and supportive relationship.

* If you feel unable to speak to your sibling, try chatting to your parents or a trusted friend about your concerns. Be calm and honest. Your parents might not even realize the seriousness of the situation and that they're fueling the rivalry with seemingly unequal treatment or comments.

* Let your parents know that it upsets you when they shower your sibling with compliments while openly criticizing your efforts. Tell them you take what they say to heart so they realize they need to think more carefully about what they might regard as throwaway comments. Alerting them to what's happening will hopefully lead to a positive change and a more peaceful home for all of you.

* Once things have calmed down, try to initiate spending some time with your sibling. Do you know what's going on in their life right now? Is there something you could do together or share that might make you like and understand one another better? A sibling can be annoying, but also one of your greatest friends.

SHARED FEELINGS

Discussing your problems may feel like a big step but you'll probably discover your sibling isn't that bad. It could be they're equally as tired and bored with the fighting. Their meanness may even stem from their jealousy of you and a perception that you're the favored one in the family.

With luck, you'll be able to channel your competitive spirits into positive endeavors—consider what Venus and Serena Williams have achieved in tennis, for example. They have won competitions both as individuals and playing together as a team.

Remember sibling rivalry is a regular part of growing up—and it's likely your brother or sister has been feeling the same way as you all along. Go on, give them a chance.

"The greatest thing you'll ever learn is just to love and be loved in return"

Nat King Cole

THE JOYS OF SOLITUDE

Are you an introvert in an extrovert world? If you're someone who enjoys being on your own and often find yourself in quiet places, this could be you. It's time to take the introvert/extrovert test...

DO YOU PREFER TO BE ALONE?

No one is a pure introvert or a pure extrovert. Rather, people fall somewhere along the line between the two, showing more of certain traits depending on how they respond to social situations. So what does it feel like if you tend toward the introvert end of the spectrum?

The power of silence
Have you ever wondered why some people dislike silence while others crave it? Yearning for quiet might mean you feel the intensity of the outside world more strongly, so you need to refuel and restore in a peaceful environment. It may seem inconceivable to extroverts, but time alone is the only way for introverts to quieten their mind and regain energy.

Quiet but not shy
If you're an introvert you may be quiet because you prefer to be on your own, not because you are shy (extroverts can be shy too) or because people scare you— but because they tire you. Introverts find that when they are by themselves they are recharging their energy, whereas when they are around highly stimulating environments they are being drained.

Behind the mask
It's not always easy to find solitude with such busy lives. So without realizing it, many introverts cope by putting up a wall to conserve their energy. In busy social situations they might instinctively put on a mask to disengage, conveying a go-away attitude (maybe looking bored or cold). But this is as much a defense mechanism as it is a protective shell.

Amazing traits
Nowadays being an extrovert is thought of as great because it means you're more likely to be chatty, charming, and self-assured. But try to remember that not all extroverts are loud and confident, just as not all introverts are tongue-tied and shy. And don't think that extroversion is a superior personality type. Society needs to remember that being thoughtful and quietly well-informed has lots going for it. Some of the personality traits an introvert might think are embarrassing— preferring to hide at parties, being the last to raise your hand in class—are indicators that you could be amazing.

DID YOU KNOW INTROVERTS ARE...

...more independent and creative
Even though working together with others is undeniably enriching, solitude generally makes people more productive as they can concentrate intensely for a long period of time, allowing a deeper analysis of ideas and abilities, boosting imagination and creativity.

...good decision makers
Introverts like to think carefully before taking a decision. Some may call it hesitancy, but it's more about being cautious. As well as a natural ability for introspection, they are also observant, making their advice most valuable.

...deep thinkers
Chit-chat with strangers is generally a no-no—small talk is seen as meaningless and boring. On the other hand, introverts relish and enjoy deep conversations with friends and family as a way to understand more about themselves and others.

...good judges of character
Through acute observation and meaningful conversations, introverts also gain a better understanding of other people. Being able to recognize the subtle messages others convey via body language and facial expressions means they are good at reading emotions.

...better writers than speakers
All that thinking and overstimulation can mean introverts sometimes find it tricky to express themselves verbally. On screen or paper, however, they have the ability to write with depth and clarity, thanks to those superior observation skills, which often give them a 360-degree view of things.

ARE YOU AN INTROVERT OR EXTROVERT?

Check the traits that best describe you:

Introverts are more likely to...
- ☐ Be reserved and cautious
- ☐ Enjoy a calm environment
- ☐ Listen more than talk
- ☐ Think then act
- ☐ Feel comfortable being alone
- ☐ Prefer to be in the background
- ☐ Have good concentration
- ☐ Prefer to focus on one thing at a time

Extroverts are more likely to...
- ☐ Be outgoing and confident
- ☐ Enjoy a vibrant environment
- ☐ Talk more than listen
- ☐ Act then think
- ☐ Feel alive being around people
- ☐ Prefer to be in the spotlight
- ☐ Be easily distracted
- ☐ Prefer to do many things at once

LOOK AGAIN

Notions of beauty vary all over the world, but the truth is that it's what's on the inside that really matters—kindness, a generous spirit, a smart brain—and that's what makes everyone uniquely beautiful

There's been a welcome change in recent years about how women are represented in the media. And thankfully, models with perfect makeup, petite waists, and impossibly long legs are no longer the only kind of women you'll see. Today, a look at your favorite Instagram™ accounts or fashion magazines will increasingly show a fabulous diversity of all shapes and sizes. It's still possible to experience feelings of inadequacy, though, with thoughts popping up like:

"I don't look like that, and I'm never going to look like that."

The wonderful truth, however, is you don't need to look like anyone other than yourself. Physical beauty is subjective—what one person finds beautiful might be very different to someone else.

In Japan, for example, a larger nose is considered handsome, while on the Indian Ocean island of Mauritius, the bigger you are, the better. To demonstrate this shifting perception of beauty, Superdrug™, a British drugstore chain, asked female graphic designers from 18 different countries to manipulate a woman's image by making her "more attractive to the people of their country."

The results were staggering. In Italy, she was made taller and thinner; in Spain they made her larger and curvier; in China, she was made to look like a Barbie™ doll; in the Netherlands they gave her red hair; and in Egypt, her hair turned jet black. No single image looked the same, and none could be called "equal" to any other.

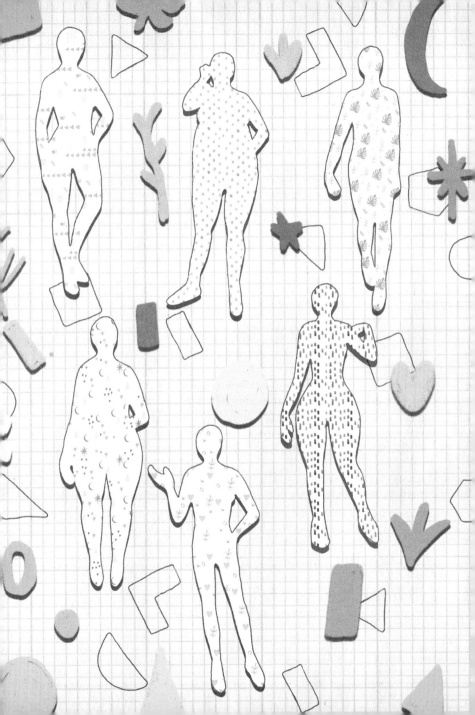

Beauty through the ages

The same is true of history. Some of the earliest known representations of a woman's body are the Venus figurines—small statues from Europe dating back 25,000 years. These squat, large-breasted, large-stomached women are thought to represent the ideal of beauty at that time.

Fast forward several thousand years to the 17th and 18th centuries, and artists continued to portray women as curvy. Flemish painter Peter Paul Rubens became known for it, and the voluptuous women he portrayed—known as Rubenesque—were held up as symbols of beauty. Nowadays, some would consider these female bodies to be "too large." Yet what was considered beautiful in the 1970s—super-skinny women without much shape—would today be thought of as "too thin." The same goes for short hair, long hair, freckles, tattoos, being "too muscular," "too short," and "too tall." There was a time when gapped teeth were thought of as "ugly"; yet some of the world's best-known models, like Lara Stone, rock the gap tooth with pride. Everyone's different, but different is what makes you individual.

It's an inside job

The trouble is, with selfies and social media, it's hard to escape the judgment of others. This makes everyone feel insecure, including those you'd expect to be confident. Even actress Margot Robbie, who's been named as one of the most beautiful women in Hollywood, said in an interview with *Vanity Fair*: "I am definitely not the best looking. I did not grow up feeling like I was particularly attractive. You should have seen me at 14, with braces and glasses, gangly and doing ballet!"

Similarly, Oscar-winning actress Lupita Nyong'o, who starred in the recent *Star Wars* movies, said in a speech about her childhood: "I put on the TV and only saw white, pale skin. I was teased and taunted about my night-shaded skin and my one prayer to God was that I would wake up light-skinned."

What's important to know is that beauty is about more than physical appearance. It's how you think, and how you behave. So be confident in yourself, because confidence is the most beautiful quality of all.

"Beauty is not in the face;
beauty is a light in the heart"

Kahlil Gibran

HOW TO HAVE MORE CONFIDENCE IN YOUR APPEARANCE

* **Look for your own positives** It might feel silly but say out loud the things you like about yourself. Maybe you have a great sense of humor, perhaps you are thoughtful of others, or do you have a nice smile? Reminding yourself of all your good points is sure to boost your confidence.

* **Find the positives in differences** Is that scar on your arm the result of an adventure? Seeing the good, even in the bits of your body you don't like so much—be that your nose, legs, or hair color—will leave you feeling happier.

* **Learn to give and accept compliments** Almost everyone feels insecure at some stage, so start saying nice things to your friends. Tell them you love their new hairstyle or you're proud of their softball skills. It will make them smile and make you happy, too. And if someone pays you a compliment, don't just brush it off. Accept it graciously.

* **Smile more** People who smile and appear happy are often perceived as warmer, friendlier people. It also improves your mood.

* **Fake it until you make it** It might be a cliché but it works. Have confidence in yourself, even when you aren't feeling your best. Over time, it'll become natural and others will take note.

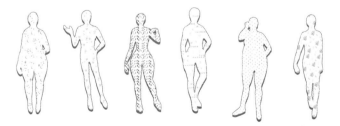

BETTER BODY IMAGE

No one is perfect, so stop being unkind to yourself and learn to love your body, quirks and all

How do you feel when you look in the mirror? Do you find yourself criticizing little details or complaining "I'm too fat" or "I'm too short" or "if only I had a different nose/butt/hair color I'd be happy"?

If you're frequently making negative comments about your appearance, you're not alone. You can be confident that most of your peers will be equally as critical of their looks, especially given all the physical changes that happen as you get older. But while it's normal not to like every part of yourself, for some it becomes so extreme it affects everyday life. This is because body image—how you see your face and body—is closely linked to self-esteem. If you aren't happy with your body, you will lack confidence. If you have a positive body image, however, you will be happier and healthier both mentally and physically.

WHAT AFFECTS HOW YOU SEE YOURSELF?

Shapeshifting As you mature, your body shape changes in ways you may and may not like. Hormones can also make you feel more sensitive and self-conscious about your appearance as you want to fit in, be accepted, and carve your own identity.

Friends and family Without realizing it, you become influenced by your friends as they also change and start wearing makeup, having different hairstyles, and clothes. You may want to be like them or create your own style—but it can get you down if you start comparing yourself to them. Remember, everyone is different. People are also quick to judge on appearance and if you're sensitive, anyone who comments on your looks can also influence your self-esteem.

Social media Think how many friends post images of themselves on social media for others to "like" or comment on. How people react to photos can have a huge impact on body image and self-confidence. If someone responds with a mean comment it could negatively affect the person, even if it is just "banter." On the other hand, 100 likes could really boost their self-esteem.

Celebrities Flawless images of perfect-looking celebrities are everywhere in the media—on TV, in magazines, on social media—and can give the wrong impression of what is a "normal" shape and what the perfect person looks like. Despite knowing they are often airbrushed, these images can have a big impact on how you view yourself.

HOW TO DEAL WITH NEGATIVE COMMENTS

There will always be one person you know who, because of their own insecurities, will mock others' appearances. If you are at the receiving end of their insensitive comments, there are a few things you can do:

Ignore them Don't let this person affect your life. Hurtful comments are horrible and it's normal to be upset, but try to move forward and don't let one comment or person who doesn't matter to you prevent you from being yourself.

Talk to a friend It's good to vent to someone you trust. They can advise you on what to do as they will see the person's comments from a different perspective.

Confide in a teacher If it happens at school and is making you feel low, talk to a staff member about it so they can help resolve the problem and find ways to boost your self-esteem.

Tell the culprit If you feel it's best, tell the person who's upset you why their comment is unkind. Be calm and avoid arguing. They may not realize how hurtful they are being.

HOW TO IMPROVE SELF-ESTEEM AND BODY IMAGE

1 Accept your amazing self and stop comparing your features to other people's

This is you—unique, wonderful you—and your body, face, and glow. In real life, very few people fit into the airbrushed, picture-perfect ideal in the media, so instead of worrying what's wrong with you, focus on what's right. This is your body, so make the most of it.

2 Silence your inner critic

Whenever you become aware you're thinking negative thoughts about yourself, say "stop." Imagine what advice you'd give to a friend or young child who was putting themselves down and pay heed to these wise words. You wouldn't suggest they be unkind to themselves.

3 Compliment yourself

Each day, look in the mirror and focus on something you like. It could be your eye color, your skin, your smile. Pay yourself a compliment instead of being harsh on yourself as this will boost your mood. You may fake positive comments to start with, but stick with it as eventually you'll start noticing they come naturally.

4 Change what you can—accept what you can't

If there is something you really dislike and can easily change— such as a hairstyle, makeup, skin cream for pimples, or exercising for health reasons—do it. But do remember that real people aren't perfect.

5 Remind yourself of what's important—who you are

If you're a good-hearted, kind person and you're healthy and fit, that's way more important than looks. Everyone has body issues at some point—it's part of life—but clichéd as it sounds, it really is what's inside that counts.

STERLING
New York

An Imprint of Sterling Publishing Co., Inc.
1166 Avenue of the Americas
New York, NY 10036

ISBN 978-1-4549-3646-6

Distributed in Canada by Sterling Publishing Co., Inc.
c/o Canadian Manda Group, 664 Annette Street
Toronto, Ontario M6S 2C8, Canada

For information about custom editions, special sales, and premium and corporate purchases, please contact Sterling Special Sales at 800-805-5489 or specialsales@sterlingpublishing.com

Manufactured in Turkey

2 4 6 8 10 9 7 5 3 1

sterlingpublishing.com

Editorial: Susie Duff, Catherine Kielthy, Jane Roe
Designer: Jo Chapman
Publisher: Jonathan Grogan

Words credits: Claire Blackmore, Vicky H Bourne, Karen Bray, Jenny Cockle, Susie Duff, Donna Findlay, Anne Guillot, Lauren Jarvis, Juliana Kassianos, Olivia Lee, Mollie McClelland Morris, Kate Orson, Rachel Roberts, Andy Rollé, Carol Anne Strange

Illustrations: Alamy.com, Shutterstock.com, Anieszka Banks, Claire van Heukelom, Ginnie Hsu, Maria Mangiapane, Samantha Nickerson, Sara Thielker, Rose Wong

Cover illustration: Sara Thielker